DEFENSE, SECURITY AND STRATEGIES

MARITIME SUPPLY CHAIN SECURITY

HIGH-RISK CARGO AND FOREIGN PORT ISSUES

DEFENSE, SECURITY AND STRATEGIES

Additional books in this series can be found on Nova's website under the Series tab.

Additional e-books in this series can be found on Nova's website under the e-book tab.

DEFENSE, SECURITY AND STRATEGIES

MARITIME SUPPLY CHAIN SECURITY

HIGH-RISK CARGO AND FOREIGN PORT ISSUES

DOLORES G. ORTEGA
EDITOR

nova publishers
New York

Library of Congress Cataloging-in-Publication Data

ISBN: 978-1-63482-777-5

Published by Nova Science Publishers, Inc. † New York

CONTENTS

PREFACE

This book discusses how many maritime shipments CBP determined to be high risk and the extent to which CBP has accurate data on the disposition of such shipments; the extent to which CBP consistently applies criteria and documents reasons for waiving examinations; and the extent to which CBP ensures its policies on the disposition of high-risk shipments are being followed. Furthermore, this book addresses the extent to which Department of Homeland Security (DHS) has assessed foreign ports that pose the greatest risk to the global supply chain and focused its maritime container security programs to address those risks; and actions DHS has taken to help ensure the efficiency and effectiveness of its maritime security programs.

Chapter 1 – The U.S. economy is dependent on a secure global supply chain. In fiscal year 2013, approximately 12 million maritime cargo shipments arrived in the United States. Within the federal government, CBP is responsible for administering cargo security, to include identifying "high-risk" maritime cargo shipments with the potential to contain terrorist contraband. GAO was asked to review CBP's disposition of such shipments. This report discusses (1) how many maritime shipments CBP determined to be high risk and the extent to which CBP has accurate data on the disposition of such shipments, (2) the extent to which CBP consistently applies criteria and documents reasons for waiving examinations, and (3) the extent to which CBP ensures its policies on the disposition of high-risk shipments are being followed. GAO analyzed CBP data on maritime shipments arriving in the United States during fiscal years 2009 through 2013. GAO also visited four CBP targeting units selected on the basis of the percentage of maritime shipments they waived, among other factors.

Chapter 2 – Foreign ports and the cargo carried by vessels from these ports are critical to the U.S. economy, but can be exploited by terrorists. Within DHS, CBP and the Coast Guard are responsible for maritime security. Through CSI, CBP identifies and examines U.S.-bound cargo that may conceal WMD, and through C-TPAT, CBP partners with international trade community members to secure the flow of U.S.-bound goods. Under the IPS program, Coast Guard officials visit foreign ports to assess compliance with security standards. GAO was asked to review DHS's maritime security programs. This report addresses (1) the extent to which DHS has assessed the foreign ports that pose the greatest risk to the global supply chain and focused its maritime container security programs to address those risks, and (2) actions DHS has taken to help ensure the efficiency and effectiveness of its maritime security programs. GAO analyzed DHS risk models and maritime security program strategies, met with program officials, and visited six foreign countries selected on the basis of participation in CSI, varied cargo shipment risk levels, and other factors.

In: Maritime Supply Chain Security
Editor: Dolores G. Ortega

ISBN: 978-1-63482-777-5

Chapter 1

SUPPLY CHAIN SECURITY: CBP NEEDS TO ENHANCE ITS GUIDANCE AND OVERSIGHT OF HIGH-RISK MARITIME CARGO SHIPMENTS*

United States Government Accountability Office

ABBREVIATIONS

ATS	Automated Targeting System
CBP	U.S. Customs and Border Protection
CERTS	Cargo Enforcement Reporting and Tracking System
CSI	Container Security Initiative
C-TPAT	Customs-Trade Partnership Against Terrorism
DHS	Department of Homeland Security
GPRA	Government Performance and Results Act
NII	nonintrusive inspection
OFO	Office of Field Operations
SAFE Port Act	Security and Accountability for Every Port Act

* This is an edited, reformatted and augmented version of a report, GAO-15-294, issued by the Government Accountability Office, dated January 2015.

Why GAO Did This Study

The U.S. economy is dependent on a secure global supply chain. In fiscal year 2013, approximately 12 million maritime cargo shipments arrived in the United States. Within the federal government, CBP is responsible for administering cargo security, to include identifying "high-risk" maritime cargo shipments with the potential to contain terrorist contraband. GAO was asked to review CBP's disposition of such shipments.

This report discusses (1) how many maritime shipments CBP determined to be high risk and the extent to which CBP has accurate data on the disposition of such shipments, (2) the extent to which CBP consistently applies criteria and documents reasons for waiving examinations, and (3) the extent to which CBP ensures its policies on the disposition of high-risk shipments are being followed.

GAO analyzed CBP data on maritime shipments arriving in the United States during fiscal years 2009 through 2013. GAO also visited four CBP targeting units selected on the basis of the percentage of maritime shipments they waived, among other factors.

What GAO Recommends

GAO recommends, among other things, that CBP define standard exception waiver categories and disseminate policy on documenting articulable reason waivers. Further, CBP should enhance its methodology for selecting shipments for self-inspections and change the way it calculates the compliance rate. The Department of Homeland Security concurred with GAO's recommendations.

What GAO Found

From fiscal years 2009 through 2013, less than 1 percent of maritime shipments arriving in the United States were identified as high risk by U.S. Customs and Border Protection (CBP), but CBP does not have accurate data on their disposition (i.e., outcomes). CBP officials (targeters) are generally required to hold high-risk shipments for examination unless evidence shows that an examination can be waived per CBP policy. In particular, targeters at

Advance Targeting Units (targeting units)—responsible for reviewing shipments arriving at ports within their respective regions—can waive an examination if they determine through research that (1) the shipment falls within a predetermined category (standard exception), or (2) they can articulate why the shipment should not be considered high risk (articulable reason), such as an error in the shipment's data. GAO found that CBP examined the vast majority of high-risk shipments, but CBP's disposition data are not accurate because of various factors—such as the inclusion of shipments that were never sent to the United States—and that the data overstate the number of high-risk shipments. On the basis of GAO's analyses and findings, CBP is taking steps to correct its data.

When determining the disposition of high-risk shipments, CBP's targeting units are inconsistently applying criteria to make waiver decisions and are incorrectly documenting the reasons for some waivers. CBP policy lacks definitions for standard exception waivers. As a result, targeters are inconsistently applying and recording standard exception waivers. Because of these inconsistencies, some targeting units may be unnecessarily holding shipments for examination, while others may be waiving shipments that should be examined. Developing definitions for standard exceptions could help ensure that CBP examines shipments as intended. Further, some targeters at targeting units GAO visited were unaware of the guidance on articulable reason waivers and were incorrectly documenting these waivers. As a result, CBP cannot accurately determine the extent to which articulable waivers are being issued and used judiciously per CBP policy. Updating and disseminating guidance in policy could help ensure targeters correctly document such waivers.

CBP has efforts in place, such as self-inspections, to provide oversight of its policies on the disposition (whether examined or waived) of high-risk shipments; however, these efforts are not sufficient. For example, the limited sample size of shipments used in self-inspections does not provide CBP with the best estimate of compliance at the national level. In addition, CBP's method for calculating the compliance rate does not accurately reflect compliance because it is not based on the number of shipments sampled. Developing an enhanced methodology for selecting sample shipments, and changing the method for calculating compliance, could improve CBP's estimate of compliance and its ability to identify and correct deficiencies.

This is a public version of a sensitive report that GAO issued in November 2014. It does not include details that CBP deemed sensitive security information.

* * *

January 27, 2015

The Honorable Bennie G. Thompson
Ranking Member
Committee on Homeland Security House of Representatives

Dear Mr. Thompson:

The U.S. economy is dependent on the expeditious flow of millions of tons of cargo each day through the global supply chain—the flow of goods from manufacturers to retailers. According to the U.S. Department of Transportation, the majority of U.S. imports arrive by ocean vessel.[1] In fiscal year 2013, approximately 12 million cargo shipments arrived at U.S. seaports from foreign ports. Criminal or terrorist attacks using cargo shipments can cause disruptions to the supply chain and can limit global economic growth and productivity.[2] Within the federal government, U.S. Customs and Border Protection (CBP), part of the Department of Homeland Security (DHS), is responsible for administering cargo security and reducing the vulnerabilities associated with the supply chain. According to DHS, balancing security concerns with the need to facilitate the free flow of commerce, part of CBP's mission, remains an ongoing challenge.[3]

CBP has developed a layered security strategy that uses a risk-based approach to focus its limited resources on targeting and examining high-risk cargo shipments that could pose a risk while allowing other cargo shipments to proceed without unduly disrupting commerce arriving in the United States. CBP's layered security strategy is based on programs that include, among other things, analyzing information to identify shipments that may be at high risk of transporting weapons of mass destruction or other contraband, working with foreign governments to examine U.S.- bound high-risk shipments at foreign ports participating in the Container Security Initiative (CSI), and providing benefits to companies that comply with predetermined security measures through the Customs-Trade Partnership Against Terrorism (C-TPAT) program. In October 2006, Congress passed and the President signed the Security and Accountability for Every Port Act (SAFE Port Act) of 2006, establishing a statutory framework for key programs within CBP's layered security strategy that previously had been CBP initiatives not specifically required by law.[4] A brief description of the core programs that constitute CBP's layered security strategy is provided in appendix I.

An important element of CBP's layered security strategy is obtaining advance cargo information to help identify shipments that are potentially high risk for containing terrorist contraband. CBP's disposition options (i.e., outcomes) for high-risk shipments include examinations or waivers. According to CBP policy, high-risk shipments are to be examined, at a minimum, by radiation detection and nonintrusive inspection (NII) equipment. [5] However, the policy also allows CBP to waive examination of a high-risk shipment if it meets certain criteria. Specifically, CBP officials at ports can waive an examination if they determine through research that (1) the shipment falls within a predetermined category of stated exceptions (standard exception), or (2) they can articulate why the shipment should not be considered high risk (articulable reason). For example, a shipment could be identified as high risk because it is associated with a shipper on a terrorist watch list, but through further research, CBP officials determine the shipper is not a true match to the terrorist watch list and, therefore, the shipment should not be considered high risk.

In response to your request, we reviewed CBP's disposition of high-risk maritime shipments in recent years. Specifically, this report addresses the following objectives:

1. How many maritime shipments arriving in the United States from fiscal years 2009 through 2013 did CBP determine to be high risk and to what extent does CBP have accurate data on the disposition of each of those high-risk shipments?
2. To what extent is CBP consistently applying standards and documenting reasons for waiving examinations of high-risk shipments?
3. To what extent does CBP ensure that its policies on the disposition of high-risk shipments are being followed?

This report is a public version of a prior sensitive report that we provided to you. CBP deemed some of the information in the prior report sensitive security information (SSI), which must be protected from public disclosure.[6] Therefore, this report omits sensitive information regarding the specific number of shipments examined and waived, and data reliability issues, among other things. The information provided in this report is more limited in scope, as it excludes such sensitive information, but it addresses the same questions as the sensitive report and the overall methodology used for both reports is the same.

To determine the number of maritime shipments arriving in the United States that CBP determined to be high risk, we obtained and analyzed data from CBP on the number of shipments and high-risk shipments, by seaport, during fiscal years 2009 through 2013—the 5 most recent fiscal years for which full-year data were available at the time of our review. To determine the extent to which CBP has accurate data on the disposition of each high-risk shipment, we analyzed CBP's data to determine the number of high-risk shipments examined and waived, as well as those shipments not examined/not waived. We then reviewed the data for obvious errors, discussed how the data were compiled with CBP officials, and determined the accuracy of a subset of both waived and not examined/not waived shipments from CBP's fiscal year 2013 data by further researching the disposition of each selected shipment with the assistance of CBP officials. We determined that the data (1) were not sufficiently reliable at the seaport level because not all shipments were associated with the correct seaport where shipments were unloaded, and (2) as discussed later in this report, contain errors that affect their reliability for calculating the number of high-risk shipments and their disposition. We did determine, though, that the data are sufficiently reliable to illustrate the overall disposition of all high-risk shipments by category—examined, waived, and not examined/not waived. We analyzed data we received from CBP's Fines, Penalties, and Forfeitures Division on "gate outs"—cargo targeted for terrorism or enforcement reasons that is released from CBP custody and departs a port without authorization or examination—for fiscal years 2009 through 2013 in order to determine the frequency of gate out occurrences relative to the overall number of not waived/not examined shipments. We discussed the process for collecting and recording gate out data with CBP officials from the Fines, Penalties, and Forfeitures Division and determined that the gate out data were sufficiently reliable for reporting the number of gate out occurrences.

To determine the extent to which CBP is consistently applying standards and documenting reasons for waiving examinations of high-risk shipments, we analyzed CBP's data on high-risk shipment waivers during fiscal year 2013, reviewed CBP policies and guidance for waiving examinations of high-risk shipments, and observed and discussed waiver practices at the Advance Targeting Units (targeting units) we visited.[7] We conducted site visits to four targeting units that appeared to issue the greatest percentage of waivers relative to the total high-risk maritime cargo shipments that arrived at their respective seaports in fiscal year 2013.[8] Although the results from our visits to these four targeting units are not generalizable to all targeting units, the visits allowed us to understand whether waiver documentation practices are consistent across these targeting units, and how such practices affect the reliability of CBP's disposition data. In order to determine whether targeting units were consistently using uniform criteria when applying standard exception waivers to high-risk shipments, we asked CBP officials at each targeting unit we visited to (1) define certain standard exception waivers listed in CBP's *National Maritime Targeting Policy*, and (2) comment on their awareness of any existing CBP guidance regarding standard exceptions.[9] We compared CBP's practices relative to standard exception waivers against standards *in Standards for Internal Control in the Federal Government*.[10] We also spoke with CBP targeting unit officials about their processes and practices for reviewing, approving, and documenting articulable reason waivers for high-risk shipments. We compared the processes and practices they use with CBP's policy for approving such waivers in the *National Maritime Targeting Policy* and CBP's guidance on documenting articulable reason waivers as prescribed in a February 2007 memorandum.[11]

In order to determine the extent to which CBP ensures that its policies on the disposition of high-risk shipments are being followed, we met with CBP officials at both headquarters and targeting units responsible for the management of high-risk maritime shipments and discussed their oversight of CBP's policies. We also met with officials from CBP's Office of Field Operations (OFO) to discuss their design and implementation of the Self-Inspection Program for sea cargo targeting, including the shipment sample size used to assess compliance and method for calculating compliance. In addition, we reviewed CBP reports summarizing the results of self-inspections, including the compliance rate and individual reports submitted by the four targeting units we visited. We then compared CBP's methodology for conducting self-inspections with best practices outlined in guidance on design evaluations. [12] Further, we reviewed quarterly reports produced by CBP outlining the disposition of high-risk shipments and discussed how these reports are used to determine whether CBP is meeting a Government Performance and Results Act (GPRA) performance goal with officials from OFO. Finally, we compared CBP's efforts to assess the accuracy of its data used for GPRA with standards in *Standards for Internal Control in the Federal Government*.[13] Additional details regarding our scope and methodology are provided in appendix II.

We conducted this performance audit from January 2014 through January 2015 in accordance with generally accepted government auditing standards.

Those standards require that we plan and perform the audit to obtain sufficient, appropriate evidence to provide a reasonable basis for our findings and conclusions based on our audit objectives. We believe that the evidence obtained provides a reasonable basis for our findings and conclusions based on our audit objectives.

BACKGROUND

Identifying High-Risk Shipments

Through what is referred to as the 24-hour rule, CBP generally requires vessel carriers to electronically transmit cargo manifests to CBP 24 hours before cargo is loaded onto U.S.-bound vessels at foreign ports.[14] Through the Importer Security Filing and Additional Carrier Requirements (known as the 10+2 rule), CBP requires importers and vessel carriers to provide data elements for improved identification of cargo shipments that may pose a risk for terrorism.[15] Importers are responsible for supplying CBP with 10 shipping data elements—such as country of origin—24 hours prior to loading, while vessel carriers are required to provide 2 data elements—container status messages and stow plans—that are not required by the 24-hour rule.[16]

The data provided by carriers and importers in compliance with the 24-hour rule and the 10+2 rule are automatically fed into CBP's Automated Targeting System (ATS)—an enforcement and decision support system that compares cargo and conveyance information against intelligence and other law enforcement data. ATS consolidates data from various sources to create a single, comprehensive record for each U.S.-bound shipment. Among other things, ATS uses a set of rules that assess different factors in the data to determine the risk level of a shipment. One set of rules within ATS, referred to collectively as the maritime national security weight set, is programmed to check for information or patterns that could be indicative of suspicious or terrorist activity. Each rule in the set has a specific weight value assigned to it, and for each risk factor that the rules identify, the weight values are added together to calculate an overall risk score for the shipment. ATS assesses and generates risk scores for every cargo shipment as the shipment moves throughout the global supply chain and new data are provided or existing data are revised. CBP classifies the risk scores from the maritime national security weight set as low, medium, or high risk. Shipments with connections to known or suspected terrorists, as well as those that include invalid information, are more likely to be classified as high risk; and shipments from shippers who participate in CBP's C-TPAT program, or "trusted shippers," are more likely to be classified as low risk. Because ATS collects and presents data on shipments, CBP targets shipments—rather than individual containers—for examination.[17]

Targeting High-Risk Shipments

ATS automatically places high-risk shipments on hold, and CBP officials (targeters) use information in ATS to identify (target) which high-risk shipments should be examined or waived.[18] If a shipment is held for examination, a CBP Anti-Terrorism Contraband Enforcement Team (enforcement team) is to conduct the examination, which is to include scanning the cargo with NII equipment, among other things.[19] Enforcement team officials are to review the images produced with the NII equipment to detect anomalies or shielding that could indicate the presence of weapons of mass destruction or other contraband. If an anomaly is detected, the shipment is to be transferred to a centralized examination station and the contents of the container are to be removed and physically examined. If contraband is discovered during the physical examination, the shipment is to be seized by CBP; otherwise it is to be released. The enforcement team is responsible for recording the examinations it conducts, as well as the results, in the Cargo Enforcement Reporting and Tracking System (CERTS)—a module within ATS.

Examinations of high-risk shipments can be waived if a CBP targeter determines that a high-risk shipment meets a "standard exception" or an "articulable reason." [20] CBP policy lists the standard exceptions to mandatory examinations.[21] Waivers based on articulable reasons are issued for reasons other than the standard exception categories. If a CBP targeter conducts analysis of available information on a high-risk shipment and determines there is no security risk, he or she is to seek approval from the port director or his/her designee(s) and record the waiver reason in CERTS within ATS. Figure 1 depicts possible targeting outcomes for high-risk shipments.

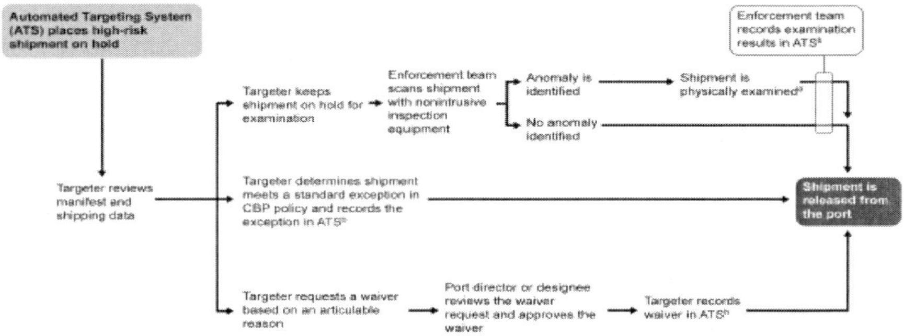

Source: GAO analysis of CBP documents. | GAO-15-294.

[a] If contraband is discovered during the physical examination, the shipment is to be seized by CBP.

[b] Examinations and waivers are recorded in the Cargo Enforcement Reporting and Tracking System (CERTS)—a module within ATS.

Figure 1. Flow Chart Depicting U.S. Customs and Border Protection's (CBP) Targeting Outcomes for High-Risk Shipments.

In addition to obtaining manifest and shipping data (e.g., 10+2 data), CBP requires the importers of goods to file entry documents so CBP can assess and collect duties. Data provided in the entry documents are assessed by ATS and can result in a shipment's risk score previously classified as low or medium risk based on manifest and shipping data to become high risk. Entry documents can also have the opposite effect. For example, entry information can confirm an entity is a C-TPAT member and, therefore, drop the shipment's score below the high-risk threshold.

Entry documents can be provided several days after a shipment's arrival in the United States and after a shipment leaves the port.[22]

Advance Targeting Units

CBP targeters are assigned to targeting units located at or near selected domestic ports, and their targeting efforts are focused on shipments destined for ports within their respective regions. A targeting unit may be responsible for targeting shipments arriving at one port or multiple ports in its region. For example, targeters at the Port of Newark are also responsible for targeting shipments that are bound for ports in New York. CBP targeters at targeting units can review data as soon as carriers and importers submit the required data (in accordance with the 24-hour rule and the 10+2 rule), and the data are available in ATS. Once a shipment is loaded onto a U.S.-bound vessel, CBP targeters continue to review shipment data in ATS because shipment data can be updated with additional or amended information. Targeters use other sources, such as public records, open sources (e.g., Internet search engines), U.S. government systems, and local port knowledge to assess whether the shipment poses a high risk or whether the risk can be mitigated based on research.

100 Percent Scanning and Prior GAO Work

In August 2007, the Implementing Recommendations of the 9/11 Commission Act of 2007 (9/11 Commission Act) was enacted, which required, among other things, that by July 2012, 100 percent of U.S.- bound cargo containers be scanned at foreign ports with both radiation detection and NII equipment before being placed on U.S.-bound vessels.[23] In May 2012, the then secretary of homeland security authorized a 2-year extension (until July 2014) of the deadline for implementing the requirement.[24] In May 2014, the Secretary of Homeland Security renewed the extension (until July 2016) and stated that "DHS's ability to fully comply with this unfunded mandate of 100 percent scanning, even in [the] long term, is highly improbable, hugely expensive, and in our judgment, not the best use of taxpayer resources to meet this country's port security and homeland security needs." The Secretary also stated that he instructed DHS, including CBP, to do a better job of meeting the underlying objectives of the 100 percent scanning requirement by, in part, refining aspects of CBP's layered security strategy.

We have previously reported on the challenges CBP faces in implementing the 100 percent scanning requirement. [25] In October 2009, we recommended, among other things, that CBP conduct feasibility and cost-benefit analyses of implementing the 100 percent scanning requirement and provide the results to Congress along with any suggestions of cost-effective alternatives to implementing the 100 percent scanning requirement, as appropriate. CBP partially concurred with the recommendations but did not implement them. We have also reported on the programs that compose CBP's layered security strategy. Specifically, we have reviewed CBP's efforts to collect additional data through the 10+2 rule and utilize these data to identify high-risk shipments;[26] examine high-risk shipments before they depart CSI ports;[27] and validate security measures taken by C-TPAT members.[28] We made several recommendations in these reports, including that CBP establish milestones and time frames for including 10+2 data in its criteria used in the identification of high-risk shipments. In December 2010, CBP provided us with a project plan for integrating the data into its criteria, and in early 2011, CBP implemented the updates to address risk factors present in the 10+2 data.

Less than 1 Percent of Arriving Maritime Shipments from Fiscal Years 2009 through 2013 Were High Risk, but CBP Does Not Have Accurate Data on Their Disposition

We determined that less than 1 percent of the maritime shipments arriving in the United States from fiscal years 2009 through 2013 were high risk; however, CBP does not have accurate data on the number and disposition of each high-risk shipment because of various factors. On the basis of our analyses, CBP's data overstate the number of high-risk shipments, including those not examined/not waived. CBP is taking steps to improve its data on the disposition of high-risk shipments.

Percentage of High-Risk Shipments Is Very Low and CBP Has Examined the Vast Majority

On the basis of our analyses of CBP data for fiscal years 2009 through 2013, on average each year, approximately 11.6 million maritime shipments arrived in the United States, and less than 1 percent of those were determined by ATS to be high risk based on the maritime national security weight set. CBP, on average, examined the vast majority of these high-risk shipments, with less than 10 percent waived or not examined/not waived.[29]

CBP Does Not Have Accurate Data on the Disposition of All High-Risk Shipments

The numbers and percentages discussed above represent CBP's data on the number of high-risk shipments and their disposition, but our analyses suggest that CBP does not have accurate data on the disposition of each high-risk shipment because of various factors.[30] In particular, CBP's data overstate the number of high-risk shipments, including those not examined/not waived. On the basis of our analysis of selected waived shipments, CBP's data may also overstate the number of waived shipments since not all shipments identified as waived were waived, but we were unable to determine the full extent to which some shipments identified as not waived/not examined were actually waived. CBP officials stated that the data include (1) shipments where the carrier deleted the bill of lading, meaning the shipments ultimately never arrived in the United States (referred to as deleted bills), and (2) shipments for which ATS assigned high risk scores only after entry was filed and the shipment had been released from the port. In further iterations of the data CBP provided us, CBP officials were able to identify the shipments in these two categories and therefore provide us with more accurate data on the number and disposition of high-risk shipments.

On the basis of our analyses of CBP's fiscal year 2009 through 2013 data, deleted bills and shipments' risk scores not rising above the high-risk threshold until after entry accounted for 8 percent, on average, of the high-risk shipments identified in CBP's data as waived. However, such shipments were not high-risk shipments requiring review by a targeter and therefore would not have been waived. Further, our analyses of CBP's data showed that deleted bills and risk scores not rising above the high-risk threshold until after entry accounted for 48 percent, on average, of the high-risk shipments identified in CBP's data as not examined/not waived. Therefore, nearly half of the shipments identified as not examined/not waived in CBP's data were, in fact, not high-risk shipments requiring an examination or waiver even though they were identified as such.

In addition to deleted bills and shipments with high risk scores only after entry was filed, we also identified other factors contributing to CBP not having accurate disposition data on high-risk shipments. We discussed a nonprobability sample of high-risk shipments with CBP officials at the four targeting units we visited. Specifically, we discussed two sets of shipments—40 high-risk shipments identified in CBP's data as waived, and 40 shipments identified as not examined/not waived.[31] We found that CBP did not have accurate disposition data for the 40 high-risk shipments identified as waived since 28 shipments were actually waived. For example, we determined that 3 shipments were examined, but the examinations were not recorded by CBP officials in CERTS within ATS. According to CBP officials at one targeting unit we visited, the 3 shipments were not recorded because of confusion over who was to record the examination. See table 1 for the actual disposition of the 40 high-risk shipments we analyzed that were identified in CBP's data as waived.

Table 1. Disposition of Selected High-Risk Shipments Identified as Waived, Fiscal Year 2013

Disposition	Number of shipments
Waived	28
Examined, but not recorded by officials	3
Not examined/not waived	2
Not high risk	
• Score was below threshold at time of arrival or did not rise above high-risk threshold until after arrival and entry was filed	5
• Deleted bill	2
Total	40

Source: GAO analysis of U.S. Customs and Border Protection data and information. | GAO-15-294.

We determined that of the 40 high-risk shipments identified in CBP's data as not examined/not waived, 1 should have been examined, and 1 waived. The remaining 38 shipments were incorrectly identified as not examined/not waived for various reasons, including 5 shipments that were examined or waived and properly recorded, but ATS did not link the records to the shipments. See table 2 for the actual disposition of the 40 high-risk shipments identified in CBP's data as not examined/not waived.

CBP data on gate out occurrences—cargo targeted for terrorism or enforcement that is released from CBP custody and departs a port without authorization or examination—also call into question the accuracy of CBP's disposition data on high-risk shipments identified as not examined/not waived. CBP requires ports to have a process in place for identifying gate outs and, in 2006, developed a uniform process for ports to report gate outs to CBP's OFO. According to CBP data collected through this process, the number of gate out occurrences is far less than the number of high-risk shipments identified as not examined/not waived, which would equate to a gate out. The number of not examined/not waived high-risk shipments should, in theory, be the same as the number of gate outs.

Table 2. Disposition of Selected High-Risk Shipments Identified as Not Examined/Not Waived, Fiscal Year 2013

Disposition	Number of shipments
Not examined/not waived	2
Waived or examined, but not recorded properly by officials	7
Waived or examined, but record not linked to shipment in the Automated Targeting System	5
Not high risk	
• Score was below threshold at time of arrival or did not rise above high-risk threshold until after arrival and entry was filed	16
• Deleted bill	10
Total	40

Source: GAO analysis of U.S. Customs and Border Protection data and information. I GAO-15-294.

In response to our findings, CBP officials acknowledged that the factors discussed above have contributed to CBP's data not being accurate, and they noted that CBP is taking steps to improve its data on the disposition of high-risk shipments. For example, CBP has already developed a query to identify shipments in its data that are not truly high risk at the time of arrival, including deleted bills and shipments with high risk scores only after arrival and entry is filed. CBP officials added that they are updating the *National Maritime Targeting Policy* to include the requirement that cargo examinations and waivers be recorded in CERTS within ATS since not all officials are adhering to this requirement and the policy will be finalized after we complete our review. In addition, enhancing certain oversight mechanisms, as discussed later in the report, could help address the inaccuracies in CBP's data.

CBP Targeting Units Are Not Consistently Applying and Documenting Reasons for Waiving Examinations of High-Risk Shipments

When determining the disposition of high-risk shipments, CBP's targeting units are inconsistently applying criteria to make some waiver decisions and are also incorrectly documenting the reasons for waivers. On the basis of our review of CBP policy and visits to selected targeting units, we determined that CBP has not established uniform definitions for standard exception waiver categories; some CBP officials were unaware of existing waiver guidance for articulable reason waivers; and some CBP targeters across the targeting units we visited were inconsistently and inaccurately recording waiver reasons in ATS. As a result, CBP cannot accurately determine the extent to which standard exception waivers are used consistently or whether waivers issued for articulable reasons are being used judiciously, as required by policy.

Targeting Units Have Varying Definitions of What Constitutes Certain Standard Exceptions

CBP's *National Maritime Targeting Policy* lists several standard exception waivers, and we found inconsistencies regarding how certain standard exception waiver categories are defined across the four targeting units we visited.[32] At these targeting units, we found that CBP targeters consistently review manifest and shipping data, including data provided through the 10+2 rule, to search for evidence that would indicate whether or not a shipment should be waived based on a standard exception. However, the criteria targeters at these targeting units are using to make these determinations are not uniformly established by any central CBP guidance or policy. Instead, they are developed locally by targeting unit officials primarily on the basis of their experience and institutional knowledge of the targeting process. Although CBP's *National Maritime Targeting Policy* identifies what the standard exception categories are, it does not provide definitions for what specifically constitutes the various standard exception categories.

Because of the lack of CBP-wide definitions for the standard exception categories, CBP targeters may be holding some shipments for examinations that should be waived. Alternatively, CBP targeters may also be waiving shipments that should have been examined. Differences in how frequently targeting units receive certain types of shipments may also affect the inconsistent interpretation of standard exceptions, and ultimately influence the variance seen in the proportion of high-risk shipments targeting units waive.[33]

Defining standard exception waiver categories and disseminating those definitions in policy would better allow targeting units and targeters to consistently apply criteria when making and recording waiver decisions, and could help ensure that CBP is examining shipments as intended. It is key that government agencies implement effective internal controls in order to minimize operational problems and achieve desired program results. According to *Standards for Internal Control in the Federal Government*, control activities help ensure that management's directives are carried out.[34] The control activities should be effective and efficient in accomplishing the agency's objectives. Examples of control activities include establishment and review of performance measures and indicators, accurate and timely recording of transactions and events, and appropriate documentation of transactions and internal controls. CBP officials acknowledged that establishing definitions for standard exceptions could reduce the inconsistent interpretation and documentation of standard exception waivers.

CBP Is Unable to Determine if Its Policy Addressing Articulable Reason Waivers Is Being Followed

All four of the targeting units we visited had a process in place for requesting and obtaining approvals for waivers based on articulable reasons in accordance with CBP policy. The four targeting units we visited each employed one of two different but comparable methods for reviewing and approving waivers. The first method involved the use of hard copy forms to request waivers, and the second method involved the use of e-mail requests for making waiver requests. Regardless of which method was used, each of the targeting units we visited requested and obtained waiver approvals in a manner that is consistent with CBP's *National Maritime Targeting Policy*, which states that the port director or his/her designee(s) is/are responsible for reviewing and approving high-risk shipment waiver requests based on articulable reasons.[35]

While the targeting units we visited had proper procedures in place for requesting and approving waivers, we found that CBP targeters at those targeting units are not correctly documenting waivers based on articulable reasons in accordance with CBP guidance. CBP issued a memorandum in

February 2007 that provides guidance on how targeters are to record waivers in ATS based on articulable reasons. According to that guidance, targeters are to select a specific drop-down menu option in CERTS as the reason for every articulable reason waiver they issue and then targeters are to provide comments in CERTS to support the justification for the waiver. However, during our visits to the targeting units, and on the basis of conversations we had with CBP targeters, we found that targeters' understanding of how to record waivers in CERTS within ATS varied. Our analysis of selected waived shipments (as previously discussed in this report) and discussions with CBP targeters indicate that some targeters are incorrectly recording some waiver reasons in ATS because they are not familiar with the February 2007 CBP memorandum that specifies how articulable reason waivers are to be recorded. According to a senior CBP official, the *National Maritime Targeting Policy*, which was last disseminated prior to the implementation of CERTS, has not been updated to address the process for recording articulable waivers in CERTS.

Neither we nor CBP could easily determine the full extent to which articulable waiver reasons were recorded properly because waivers based on articulable reasons cannot be segregated from waivers issued for standard exceptions. The inconsistent recording of articulable reason waivers in ATS limits CBP's ability to determine whether targeting units are following policy, since CBP's *National Maritime Targeting Policy* states that waivers based on articulable reasons are to be used "judiciously." In order to evaluate whether targeting units are judiciously making waiver decisions based on articulable reasons, CBP would need accurate records in ATS regarding the basis for why shipments were waived in order to be able to easily distinguish the two types of waivers.

In particular, CBP is reliant on targeters' selecting the appropriate waiver reasons from the drop-down menu selections in CERTS in order to be able to accurately analyze waiver data. Although the comments in the remarks section of CERTS justifying the waiver may provide further details regarding the reasons for waivers, it would be difficult for CBP to accurately determine waiver reasons on the basis of large-scale data queries of comments in the remarks section alone. Therefore, it is important for targeters to select the proper drop-down menu options when documenting waiver reasons. According to *Standards for Internal Control in the Federal Government*, management must continually assess and evaluate its internal controls to ensure that the control activities being used are effective and updated when necessary.[36] Updating and disseminating guidance in policy on how to record articulable reason waivers will help ensure that they are correctly recorded.

CBP's Mechanisms to Oversee the Implementation of Disposition Policies Could Be Enhanced

CBP has some mechanisms to provide oversight of its policies on the disposition of high-risk shipments, such as biannual self-inspections; however, these are not sufficient to fully identify whether officials are complying with policy on examinations and waivers. Further, CBP could enhance the quality of its reports on the disposition of high-risk shipments.

CBP Has Mechanisms to Determine if Its Policies Are Being Followed

CBP's OFO has mechanisms to determine if CBP policies on the disposition of high-risk shipments are being followed. Specifically, OFO monitors compliance with policies on the disposition of high-risk shipments through three efforts:

- Self-Inspection Program: OFO requires port directors (or their designees) to complete self-inspection worksheets on cargo targeting every other year to determine whether CBP officials are following policy when it comes to examining high-risk shipments and recording those examinations. In addition to reporting any deficiencies, the inspection reports sent to OFO are to include the corrective actions taken to address the deficiencies identified.
- Quarterly performance reports: CBP compiles data from ATS on high-risk shipments to measure CBP's performance in reviewing high-risk shipments in support of GPRA.[37] Among other things, the quarterly reports provide data on the number of high-risk shipments that arrived at each U.S. seaport, including the number of shipments reviewed by a targeter and the number waived.
- Monitoring gate outs: CBP requires ports to uniformly report all gate out occurrences to OFO as soon as the gate out is discovered. The

local port submits a notification worksheet to the Office of Cargo, Conveyance and Security (within OFO) that, in turn, determines if a gate out truly occurred.

However, as discussed below, we found weaknesses in some of the mechanisms CBP uses to provide oversight of its policies.

CBP Needs to Improve Oversight of Its Policies to Better Identify ATS Data Deficiencies

We found that CBP's efforts are not sufficient to identify when officials are not following policies on high-risk shipments and, subsequently, deficiencies in how data are recorded in ATS, including examinations and waivers. The Self-Inspection Program requires port directors or their designees to analyze selected shipments and complete a worksheet composed of three questions to check compliance with policies on examining high-risk shipments and recording examinations. The three worksheet questions are as follows:

1. Were cargo examination findings input within CERTS and, when appropriate, within other systems?
2. Were all shipments that received an ATS score at or above the national security threshold score placed on hold?
3. Did all shipments that received an ATS score at or above the national security threshold undergo a mandatory examination utilizing, at a minimum, an NII imaging system and screening with radiation detection technology?

The guidance provided on how to select shipments to answer the three questions, depending on the question, states that 10 percent of all shipments are to be randomly selected, with a minimum of 10 shipments and no more than 20 shipments, or 20 shipments are to be randomly selected among high-risk shipments. After port directors or their designees submit their completed worksheets, CBP OFO calculates the national compliance rate by dividing the number of worksheets that have at least 1 shipment that did not conform to policy by the total number of self-inspection worksheets submitted to OFO.

Given that the sample size is generally the same for all port directors regardless of the number of shipments their ports receive, on the basis of our analysis, the sample does not provide CBP with an efficient estimate of compliance at the national level. For example, by allocating additional samples to ports with more arriving shipments, the national compliance estimate could have a reduced sampling error. Through its Self-Inspection Program, CBP has identified a minimal number of noncompliant shipments requiring corrective action. For example, five corrective actions were taken nationwide based on the 2011 self-inspection reporting cycle, and two corrective actions based on the 2012 cycle. CBP's compliance rate was over 93 percent for both cycles, leading CBP to reduce the frequency of the self-inspections for maritime cargo targeting from every year to every other year, according to CBP OFO officials. However, as discussed previously, we determined that 3 of 40 shipments identified as waived were actually examined, but the examinations were not properly recorded and 6 of 40 shipments identified as not examined/not waived were examined or waived, but not properly recorded. Thus, CBP's compliance estimates may be overstated. CBP could improve its ability to estimate national compliance rates for maritime cargo targeting practices through different methods. For example, CBP could increase the number of shipments sampled by ports with the greatest number of arriving shipments or consider a stratified sample with strata defined in terms of size of ports and other factors that might be related to compliance or risk, such as whether shipments appear in its data as not examined/not waived. By enhancing its methodology for selecting shipment samples, CBP could better identify any deficiencies and take appropriate corrective actions. According to a Director in OFO, CBP is considering changing the shipment sample size to a percentage of high-risk shipments, which would result in port directors of larger ports analyzing a greater number of shipments than the 20 shipments per question they currently sample. However, CBP has not finalized its plans for making this change.

Further, CBP's method for calculating the compliance rate does not accurately reflect compliance nationwide because it does not calculate the rate based on the number of shipments sampled. Rather, CBP calculates the rate based on the number of worksheets that contained shipments for which policy was not followed regardless of whether it was 1 shipment or all shipments included in the worksheet. According to guidance on design evaluations, the data should be analyzed in a way that allows valid conclusions to be drawn from the evaluation.[38] CBP could improve its ability to estimate national compliance with maritime cargo targeting practices by changing its compliance rate calculation to divide the number of shipments (the unit of measure) that did not conform to policy by the total number of shipments sampled, rather than calculating the rate based on the number of worksheets.

In addition to the limited nature of the self-inspections, we also found that CBP does not fully assess the reliability of the data it analyzes on the disposition of high-risk shipments for the quarterly reports it produces in support of GPRA. Through our reliability assessment of CBP's data, we identified high-risk shipments that were not high risk and shipments for which the disposition (e.g., waived) was not recorded accurately (as previously discussed). An independent review team contracted by DHS to verify and validate the completeness and reliability of CBP's performance data used for the GPRA measure on high-risk cargo determined that CBP only addressed significant anomalies in its data contained in the quarterly reports and recommended, in May 2014, that CBP develop a formal quality control process for field data. [39] OFO concurred with the recommendation "with reservations," adding that it believed reinforcing existing policies and procedures through the local CBP command structure would address the errors. However, in CBP's data we also found errors not attributable to field data.[40]

CONCLUSION

In the absence of being able to ensure that 100 percent of U.S.-bound maritime cargo containers are scanned at foreign ports, as required by statute, the Secretary of Homeland Security has instructed DHS, including CBP, to do a better job of meeting the underlying objectives of the 100 percent scanning requirement by, in part, refining aspects of CBP's layered security strategy. Given that examining and waiving, if appropriate, high-risk shipments are critical aspects of CBP's strategy, it is important for CBP to ensure that these practices are carried out consistently and that results of its targeters' actions regarding the disposition of high-risk cargo shipments are recorded accurately. CBP is starting to take actions to correct errors in its data and revise its *National Maritime Targeting Policy*, but it needs to take further actions to ensure its policies are consistently being followed and to enhance the reliability of its high-risk shipment data. For example, without defining the standard exceptions in policy, CBP is not able to ensure that all high-risk shipments are being appropriately examined or waived. Further, without updating and disseminating policy on how to record such waivers, CBP will not be able to determine whether its targeting units are using articulable reason waivers judiciously, as called for in policy. Moreover, enhancing the methodology used in CBP's Self-Inspection Program will allow it to better identify instances where policy is not being followed and implement corrective actions. Such actions, in turn, could help CBP better ensure that its policies on the disposition of high-risk shipments are being followed.

RECOMMENDATIONS FOR EXECUTIVE ACTION

To help ensure compliance with policies on waiving high-risk shipments, we recommend that the Commissioner of CBP direct OFO to take the following two actions:

- develop a definition for each of the standard exception waiver categories and include those definitions in policy to ensure that targeting units are consistently applying those definitions when making and documenting waiver decisions in CERTS, and
- update and disseminate policy to ensure that all targeting units are correctly documenting waivers based on articulable reasons in CERTS.

To enhance oversight of the disposition of high-risk shipments—examinations and waivers—we recommend that the Commissioner of CBP direct OFO to take two actions:

- develop an enhanced methodology for selecting shipment samples used for self-inspection to increase the likelihood that any potential deficiencies will be identified so that corrective actions can be taken to reduce errors in the future, and
- develop a better national estimate of compliance with maritime cargo targeting policies by calculating the compliance rate based on individual shipments rather than worksheets.

AGENCY COMMENTS AND OUR EVALUATION

We provided a draft of the sensitive version of this report to DHS for its review and comment. DHS provided technical comments, which have been incorporated into this report, as appropriate. DHS also provided written comments. In its comments, DHS concurred with the report's four recommendations and described actions it has under way or planned to address the recommendations by June 30, 2015.

DHS concurred with the first recommendation and stated that CBP plans to develop a definition for each of the standard exception waiver categories. DHS concurred with the second recommendation and stated that CBP will provide guidance on issuing waivers based on articulable reasons in its updated *National Cargo Targeting Policy*. DHS concurred with the third recommendation and stated that CBP has updated its self-inspection worksheet for the 2015 inspection cycle in response to the recommendation. DHS concurred with the fourth recommendation and stated that CBP will develop the ability to generate reports on noncompliant high-risk shipments and require port directors or their designees to review the reports and take corrective actions based on noncompliant shipments. If implemented as planned, these actions should address the intent of the recommendations to improve CBP's disposition of high-risk shipments.

In its comments, DHS also referred to a fifth recommendation related to reviewing port codes. Because DHS deemed the details of this recommendation and its response as sensitive security information, they are not included in this public version of the report.

Sincerely yours,

Jennifer Grover, Director
Homeland Security and Justice

APPENDIX I: DESCRIPTION OF CBP'S LAYERED SECURITY STRATEGY FOR MARITIME CARGO SHIPMENTS

This appendix describes the core programs related to U.S. Customs and Border Protection's (CBP) strategy for ensuring the security of maritime cargo. CBP has developed this strategy to mitigate the risk of weapons of mass destruction, terrorist-related material, or other contraband being smuggled into the United States. CBP's strategy is based on related programs that attempt to focus resources on high-risk shipments while allowing other cargo shipments to proceed without unduly disrupting the flow of commerce into the United States. The strategy includes obtaining advanced cargo information to identify high-risk shipments, using technology to inspect cargo, and partnering with foreign governments and the trade industry. Table 3 provides a brief description of some of the core programs that compose this security strategy.

Table 3. Description of U.S. Customs and Border Protection's (CBP) Core Cargo Security Programs

Program and year introduced	Description
Obtaining advanced information to identify high-risk cargo Automated Targeting System (ATS), 1999	ATS is an enforcement and decision support system that compares traveler, cargo, and conveyance information against intelligence and other enforcement data by incorporating risk-based targeting scenarios and assessments. ATS assigns a risk score to arriving cargo shipments based on shipping information to help CBP identify and prevent potential terrorists and terrorist weapons from entering the United States.
24-hour rule, 2002	CBP generally requires vessel carriers to electronically transmit cargo manifests to CBP's Automated Manifest System 24 hours before U.S.-bound cargo is loaded onto a vessel at a foreign port. The information is used by ATS in its calculation of risk scores. The cargo manifest information is submitted by vessel carriers for all arriving cargo shipments.
Importer Security Filing and Additional Carrier Requirements (also known as the 10+2 rule), 2009	CBP requires importers and vessel carriers to provide data elements for improved identification of containerized shipments that may pose a risk for terrorism. The importer is responsible for supplying CBP with 10 shipping data elements, such as country of origin, 24 hours prior to loading, while the vessel carrier is required to provide 2 data elements, container status messages and stow plans, not required by the 24-hour rule. [a]
Domestic scanning technology deployments	
Nonintrusive inspection (NII) equipment, 2001	CBP uses NII equipment to actively scan both randomly selected containers and those identified by ATS as high risk. NII uses X-rays or gamma rays to scan a container and create images of the container's contents without opening it. According to CBP, as of August 2014, it had deployed 272 large-scale NII systems to U.S. seaports to scan containers
Radiation portal monitors, 2002	CBP's program to scan 100 percent of containers arriving in the United States with radiation detection equipment prior to leaving a domestic port. As of August 2014, the Department of Homeland Security (DHS) had deployed

Table 3. (Continued)

Program and year introduced	Description
	388 radiation portal monitors at U.S. seaports, through which over 99 percent of all containerized cargo arriving by sea is scanned.
Partnerships with foreign governments and the trade industry	
Container Security Initiative, 2002	CBP places staff at participating foreign ports to work with host country customs officials to target and examine high-risk container cargo for weapons of mass destruction before they are shipped to the United States. CBP officials identify the containers that may pose a risk for terrorism and request that their foreign counterparts examine the contents of the containers. As of July 2014, there were 58 Container Security Initiative ports located in 32 countries.
Customs-Trade Partnership Against Terrorism, 2001	CBP develops voluntary partnerships with members of the international trade community composed of importers; manufacturers; customs brokers; forwarders; air, sea, and land carriers; and contract logistics providers. Private companies that implement specific security measures and best practices receive facilitated processing, such as a reduced likelihood of security-based examinations of their cargo.

Source: GAO summary of information provided by the Department of Homeland Security. I GAO-15-294.

[a] Container status messages report terminal container movements, such as loading and discharging the vessel, and report the change in the status of containers, such as if they are empty or full. The stow plan contains the position of each cargo container on a vessel.

APPENDIX II: OBJECTIVES, SCOPE, AND METHODOLOGY

This report addresses U.S. Customs and Border Protection's (CBP) disposition of high-risk maritime cargo shipments. More specifically, our objectives were to examine (1) the number of maritime shipments arriving in the United States from fiscal years 2009 through 2013 that CBP determined to be high risk and the extent to which CBP has accurate data on the disposition of each of those high-risk shipments, (2) the extent to which CBP is consistently applying standards and documenting reasons for waiving examinations of high-risk shipments, and (3) the extent to which CBP ensures that its policies on the disposition of high-risk shipments are being followed.

To address all of these objectives, we reviewed CBP policies regarding the targeting and waiving of high-risk shipments, analyzed CBP data, and spoke with key CBP officials at both headquarters and selected targeting units. To determine the number of maritime shipments arriving in the United States that CBP determined to be high risk, we obtained data from CBP on the number of shipments and high-risk shipments that arrived in the United States by seaport during fiscal years 2009 through 2013—the 5 most recent fiscal years for which full-year data were available at the time of our review.[1] To determine the extent to which CBP has accurate data on the disposition of each high-risk shipment, we analyzed CBP's data to determine the number of high-risk shipments examined, and waived—the disposition options we identified in CBP's *National Maritime Targeting Policy*—as well as those shipments not examined/not waived.[2] We excluded foreign cargo remaining on board (FROB) shipments— cargo not discharged in the United States—from the scope of our review to focus on shipments unloaded at United States seaports. To assess the reliability of the data, we reviewed the data for obvious errors and discussed our observations with CBP officials who compiled the data. We also discussed with CBP officials how the data are entered and maintained and interviewed officials who enter the data in CBP's Automated Targeting System (ATS). We also selected a nonprobability sample of shipments from CBP's fiscal year 2013 data to determine the accuracy of the disposition data. Specifically, from the list of waived shipments in CBP's fiscal year 2013 shipment data, we selected a nonprobability sample of 40 waived shipments that represented a variety of waiver reasons recorded in ATS. We also selected a second nonprobability sample of 40 not examined/not waived shipments from the same set of data, to include shipments CBP identified as deleted bills and shipments with high-risk scores only after entry was filed. These shipment samples were associated with the four Advance Targeting Units (targeting units) we visited (see below for site visit selection criteria). We discussed the accuracy of both sample sets with targeting unit officials. We determined that CBP's data likely overstate the number of high-risk shipments, including those not examined/not waived, but the data are sufficiently reliable to illustrate the overall disposition of all high-risk shipments by category—examined, waived, and not examined/not waived—since a small percentage of shipments were waived and not examined/not waived relative to the number examined.

In addition to analyzing CBP's disposition data, we collected and analyzed gate out data for fiscal years 2009 through 2013 from CBP's Fines, Penalties, and Forfeitures Division in order to determine the frequency of gate out occurrences relative to the overall number of not waived/not examined shipments. To assess the reliability of the data, we reviewed gate out case files and assessed whether the information contained in the files matched with fiscal years 2009 through 2013 gate out data we received from CBP. We also discussed the process for collecting and recording gate out data with CBP officials from the Fines, Penalties, and Forfeitures Division. We determined that the gate out data were sufficiently reliable for reporting the number of gate out occurrences.

To determine the extent to which CBP is consistently applying standards and documenting reasons for waiving examinations of high-risk shipments, we analyzed CBP's data on high-risk shipment waivers recorded during fiscal year 2013, reviewed CBP policies and guidance on waiving examinations of high-risk shipments, and observed and discussed waiver practices at the targeting units we visited.[3] We conducted site visits to four targeting units that appeared to issue the greatest percentage of waivers relative to the total high-risk maritime cargo shipments that arrived in their respective seaports in fiscal year 2013.[4] These targeting units also represent a variety of geographical locations within the United States, as they are situated on the Gulf, East, and West Coasts. Additionally, they encompass seaports of varying sizes based on arriving shipments, ranging from approximately 146,000 shipments to 4.4 million shipments. We reviewed selected samples of waived shipments in CBP's data with officials at each targeting unit in order to gain an understanding of how targeters selected and documented waiver reasons, including standard exceptions for each of the shipments. Although the results from our visits to these four targeting units are not generalizable to all targeting units across the United States, the visits allowed us to understand whether waiver documentation practices are consistent across the targeting units we visited, and how such practices affect the reliability of CBP's disposition data.

We asked CBP officials at each targeting unit we visited to define certain standard exception waivers listed in *CBP's National Maritime Targeting Policy* in order to determine whether targeting units were consistently using uniform criteria when applying standard exception waivers to high-risk shipments. Additionally, we asked targeters to comment on their awareness of any existing CBP policy or central guidance regarding the definition of the various standard exceptions. We compared CBP's practices relative to standard exception waivers against standards in *Standards for Internal Control in the Federal Government*, which state that control activities should be effective and efficient in accomplishing the agency's objectives. [5] We spoke with CBP officials at each of the four targeting units we visited about their processes for reviewing and approving articulable reason waivers for high-risk shipments and assessed their compliance with CBP policy on approving waivers documented in the *National Maritime Targeting Policy*. At each of the four targeting units, we also met with CBP targeters to discuss and observe their practices for recording examination waivers based on articulable reasons in ATS. We then compared those practices with CBP guidance on how to record articulable reasons waivers, as prescribed in a February 2007 CBP memorandum.[6]

In order to determine the extent to which CBP ensures that its policies on the disposition of high-risk shipments are being followed, we met with CBP officials at both headquarters and targeting units responsible for the management of high-risk maritime shipments and discussed their oversight of CBP's policies. We met with officials from CBP's Office of Field Operations (OFO) to discuss their design and implementation of the Self-Inspection Program for maritime cargo targeting, including the shipment sample size used to assess compliance and method for calculating compliance. We reviewed CBP reports summarizing the results of self-inspections, including the compliance rate, as well as individual reports submitted by the four targeting units we visited. We then compared CBP's methodology for conducting self-inspections with best practices outlined in guidance on design evaluations.[7] Further, we reviewed quarterly reports produced by CBP outlining the disposition of high-risk shipments and discussed with officials from OFO how these reports are used to determine whether CBP is meeting a Government Performance and Results Act (GPRA) performance goal. We compared CBP's efforts to assess the accuracy of its data used in support of GPRA with standards in *Standards for Internal Control in the Federal Government*.[8] We also met with officials from CBP's Fines, Penalties, and Forfeitures Division to discuss CBP's procedures for identifying and reporting gate outs.

We conducted this performance audit from January 2014 through January 2015 in accordance with generally accepted government auditing standards. Those standards require that we plan and perform the audit to obtain sufficient, appropriate evidence to provide a reasonable basis for our findings and conclusions based on our audit objectives. We believe that the evidence obtained provides a reasonable basis for our findings and conclusions based on our audit objectives.

End Notes

[1] U.S. Department of Transportation, Research and Innovative Technology Administration, Bureau of Transportation Statistics, America's Container Ports: Linking Markets at Home and Abroad (Washington, D.C.: January 2011).

[2] The White House, National Strategy for Global Supply Chain Security (Washington, D.C.: January 2012).

[3] In addition to its priority mission of keeping terrorists and their weapons out of the United States, CBP is also responsible for securing the border, facilitating international trade and travel, collecting duties, and enforcing numerous U.S. laws and regulations pertaining to immigration and illicit drugs, among other things.

[4] Pub. L. No. 109-347, 120 Stat. 1884 (2006).

[5] Radiation detection equipment detects radiation being emitted from a container. Through an NII scan, CBP can identify anomalies in a container's image that could, among other things, indicate the presence of material to shield weapons of mass destruction. NII uses X-rays or gamma rays to scan a container and create images of the container's contents without having to open it.

[6] See 49 C.F.R. pt. 1520.

[7] CBP officials are assigned to targeting units located at or near select domestic ports, and their efforts at these targeting units are focused on shipments destined for ports within their respective regions.

[8] Because of issues relating to the accuracy of CBP's data that we uncovered during our site visits and therefore subsequent to developing our site visit methodology, the targeting units we visited may not actually represent the four targeting units that issued the greatest percentage of waivers relative to their total high-risk maritime cargo shipments in fiscal year 2013.

[9] U.S. Customs and Border Protection, National Maritime Targeting Policy, CBP Directive No. 3290-007B (Washington, D.C.: Dec. 28, 2007).

[10] GAO, Standards for Internal Control in the Federal Government, GAO/AIMD-00-21.3.1 (Washington, D.C.: Nov. 1, 1999).

[11] U.S. Customs and Border Protection, Authorization to Waive ATS Threshold Exams in All Transportation Modes (Washington, D.C.: Feb. 26, 2007).

[12] GAO, Designing Evaluations: 2012 Revision, GAO-12-208G (Washington, D.C.: January 2012). This report addresses the reasons to systematically plan evaluations, which include (1) enhancing their quality, credibility, and usefulness, and (2) using time and resources effectively. It is based on GAO studies and policy documents and program evaluation literature.

[13] GAO/AIMD-00-21.3.1.

[14] 19 C.F.R. § 4.7(b). Cargo manifests are prepared by the ocean carrier and are composed of bills of lading for each shipment loaded onto a vessel to describe the contents of the shipments. Bills of lading are documents issued by a carrier describing the goods, the details of the intended voyage, and the conditions of transportation.

[15] Importer Security Filing and Additional Carrier Requirements, 73 Fed. Reg. 71,730 (Nov. 25, 2008) (codified at 19 C.F.R. pts. 4, 12, 18, 101, 103, 113, 122, 123, 141, 143, 149, 178, & 192).

[16] Container status messages report terminal container movements, such as loading and discharging the vessel, and report the change in the status of containers, such as if they are empty or full. Container status messages also report conveyance movements, such as vessel arrivals and departures. A vessel stow plan includes information such as the vessel operator,

voyage number, the stow position of each container, hazardous material code (if applicable), and the port of discharge.

[17] For containerized shipments, a single shipment may consist of one or more containers, or multiple shipments may be consolidated into a single container for transport. The 12 million shipments that arrived in the United States in fiscal year 2013 included 12.6 million containers.

[18] Targeters can also use their discretion and place low- and medium-risk shipments on hold for examination.

[19] In locations where no enforcement team exists, port management assigns examinations to CBP officials within the port.

[20] Although targeters overseas at CSI ports can recommend examination waivers, for the purposes of this report, we are reviewing actions taken domestically since only domestic targeters can request waivers.

[21] Examples of standard exceptions are not included because CBP considers them to be sensitive security information.

[22] According to a senior CBP official, if the entry documents are not available until well after a shipment's arrival (e.g., after a shipment moves in bond to its final port of entry), and the score then equals or exceeds the high-risk threshold, the shipment cannot be released from the warehouse (or bonded facility) until CBP has properly mitigated the risk and changed the entry status to "released."

[23] Pub. L. No. 110-53, § 1701(a), 121 Stat. 266, 489-90 (amending 6 U.S.C. § 982(b)).

[24] The 9/11 Commission Act scanning provision includes possible extensions for containers loaded at a port or ports for which DHS certifies that at least two out of a list of specific conditions exist. Among others, these conditions include the following: (1) adequate scanning equipment is not available or cannot be integrated with existing systems, (2) a port does not have the physical characteristics to install the equipment, or (3) use of the equipment will significantly affect trade capacity and the flow of cargo. See 6 U.S.C. § 982(b)(4).

[25] GAO, Supply Chain Security: Container Security Programs Have Matured, but Uncertainty Persists over the Future of 100 Percent Scanning, GAO-12-422T (Washington, D.C.: Feb. 7, 2012), and Supply Chain Security: Feasibility and Cost-Benefit Analysis Would Assist DHS and Congress in Assessing and Implementing the Requirement to Scan 100 Percent of U.S.-Bound Containers, GAO-10-12 (Washington, D.C.: Oct. 30, 2009).

[26] GAO, Supply Chain Security: CBP Needs to Conduct Regular Assessments of Its Cargo Targeting System, GAO-13-9 (Washington, D.C.: Oct. 25, 2012), and Supply Chain Security: CBP Has Made Progress in Assisting the Trade Industry in Implementing the New Importer Security Filing Requirements, but Some Challenges Remain, GAO-10-841 (Washington, D.C.: Sept. 10, 2010).

[27] GAO, Supply Chain Security: DHS Could Improve Cargo Security by Periodically Assessing Risks from Foreign Ports, GAO-13-764 (Washington, D.C.: Sept. 16, 2013); Supply Chain Security: Examinations of High-Risk Cargo at Foreign Seaports Have Increased, but Improved Data Collection and Performance Measures Are Needed, GAO-08-187 (Washington, D.C.: Jan. 25, 2008); and Container Security: A Flexible Staffing Model and Minimum Equipment Requirements Would Improve Overseas Targeting and Inspection Efforts, GAO-05-557 (Washington, D.C.: Apr. 26, 2005).

[28] GAO, Supply Chain Security: U.S. Customs and Border Protection Has Enhanced Its Partnership with Import Trade Sectors, but Challenges Remain in Verifying Security Practices, GAO-08-240 (Washington, D.C.: Apr. 25, 2008), and Cargo Security: Partnership

Program Grants Importers Reduced Scrutiny with Limited Assurance of Improved Security, GAO-05-404 (Washington, D.C.: Mar. 11, 2005).

[29] According to CBP data, 99 percent of all high-risk shipments are reviewed by a targeter, meaning the targeter reviewed the shipments' records in ATS to identify potential threats before the shipments were loaded onto a vessel at a foreign port.

[30] We determined that CBP's data on the overall disposition of high-risk shipments— specifically those examined, waived, and not examined/not waived—may not reflect the actual disposition of the high-risk shipments since some discrepancies were found among waived and not examined/not waived high-risk shipments that represent a small percentage of high-risk shipments.

[31] Further details on the shipments we selected can be found in app. II.

[32] Examples of standard exception definitions are not included because CBP considers them to be sensitive security information.

[33] Examples of the impact of inconsistent definitions are not included because CBP considers them to be sensitive security information.

[34] GAO/AIMD-00-21.3.1.

[35] Although the policy to review and approve waiver requests does not apply to standard exception waivers, we found that standard exceptions were subject to the same review and approval process as articulable reason waivers at all four targeting units we visited.

[36] GAO/AIMD-00-21.3.1.

[37] The Government Performance and Results Act of 1993 provides the statutory framework for performance management in the federal government. Congress updated GPRA with the GPRA Modernization Act of 2010, which enhances the requirements for agencies to consult with Congress when establishing or adjusting government-wide and agency goals.

[38] GAO-12-208G.

[39] Energetics, Independent Verification and Validation of Performance Measure Data: FY 2014 Review and Report of Findings (May 2014).

[40] Details on the data errors and their impact on operations are not included because CBP considers them to be sensitive security information.

End Notes for Apendix II

[1] For the purpose of our review, a high-risk shipment is a shipment CBP's Automated Targeting System (ATS) identified as high risk based on the maritime national security weight set.

[2] U.S. Customs and Border Protection, National Maritime Targeting Policy, CBP Directive No. 3290-007B (Washington, D.C.: Dec. 28, 2007).

[3] We reviewed both types of waivers identified in the National Maritime Targeting Policy—standard exceptions and articulable reasons. Articulable waivers are requested based on discretion, whereas standard exceptions are specified in policy and not intended to be subject to interpretation.

[4] Because of issues relating to the accuracy of CBP's data that we uncovered during our site visits and therefore subsequent to developing our site visit methodology, it is possible that the targeting units we visited may not actually represent the four targeting units that issued the greatest percentage of waivers relative to their total high-risk maritime cargo shipments in fiscal year 2013.

[5] GAO/AIMD-00-21.3.1.

[6] U.S. Customs and Border Protection, Authorization to Waive ATS Threshold Exams in All Transportation Modes (Washington, D.C.: Feb. 26, 2007).

[7] GAO-12-208G.

[8] GAO/AIMD-00-21.3.1.

In: Maritime Supply Chain Security
Editor: Dolores G. Ortega

ISBN: 978-1-63482-777-5

Chapter 2

SUPPLY CHAIN SECURITY: DHS COULD IMPROVE CARGO SECURITY BY PERIODICALLY ASSESSING RISKS FROM FOREIGN PORTS*

United States Government Accountability Office

WHY GAO DID THIS STUDY

Foreign ports and the cargo carried by vessels from these ports are critical to the U.S. economy, but can be exploited by terrorists. Within DHS, CBP and the Coast Guard are responsible for maritime security. Through CSI, CBP identifies and examines U.S.-bound cargo that may conceal WMD, and through C-TPAT, CBP partners with international trade community members to secure the flow of U.S.-bound goods. Under the IPS program, Coast Guard officials visit foreign ports to assess compliance with security standards. GAO was asked to review DHS's maritime security programs. This report addresses (1) the extent to which DHS has assessed the foreign ports that pose the greatest risk to the global supply chain and focused its maritime container security programs to address those risks, and (2) actions DHS has taken to help ensure the efficiency and effectiveness of its maritime security programs.

* This is an edited, reformatted and augmented version of a United States Government Accountability Office publication, No. GAO-13-764, dated September 2013.

GAO analyzed DHS risk models and maritime security program strategies, met with program officials, and visited six foreign countries selected on the basis of participation in CSI, varied cargo shipment risk levels, and other factors.

WHAT GAO RECOMMENDS

GAO recommends that CBP periodically assess the supply chain security risks from foreign ports that ship cargo to the United States and use the results to inform any future expansion of CSI and determine whether changes need to be made to existing CSI ports. DHS concurred with GAO's recommendation.

WHAT GAO FOUND

Department of Homeland Security (DHS) components have developed models to assess the risks of foreign ports and cargo, but not all components have applied risk management principles to assess whether maritime security programs cover the riskiest ports. The U.S. Coast Guard uses its risk model to inform operational decisions for its International Port Security (IPS) program and annually updates its assessment. In contrast, U.S. Customs and Border Protection (CBP) has not regularly assessed ports for risks to cargo under its Container Security Initiative (CSI) program. CBP's selection of the initial 23 CSI ports was primarily based on the volume of U.S.-bound containers, but beginning in 2003, CBP considered more threat information when it expanded the number of CSI ports. CBP has not assessed the risk posed by foreign ports that ship cargo to the United States for its CSI program since 2005. In 2009, CBP developed a model that ranked 356 potential expansion ports for a related program on the basis of risk, but it was never implemented because of budget cuts. By applying CBP's risk model to fiscal year 2012 cargo shipment data, GAO found that CSI did not have a presence at about half of the ports CBP considered high risk, and about one fifth of the existing CSI ports were at lower risk locations. Since the CSI program depends on cooperation from sovereign host countries, there are challenges to implementing CSI in new foreign locations, and CBP's negotiations with other countries have not always succeeded. For example, CBP officials said it is difficult to close CSI ports and open new ports because removing CSI from a country might negatively affect U.S. relations with the host government.

However, periodically assessing the risk level of cargo shipped from foreign ports and using the results to inform any future expansion of CSI to additional locations, as well as determine whether changes need to be made to existing CSI ports, would help ensure that CBP is allocating its resources to provide the greatest possible coverage of high-risk cargo to best mitigate the risk of importing weapons of mass destruction (WMD) or other terrorist contraband into the United States through the maritime supply chain.

DHS has taken steps to improve the efficiency and effectiveness of its maritime security programs, but faces host country political and legal constraints. The Coast Guard has implemented a risk-informed model that prioritizes the countries to visit and assist. Also, the Coast Guard and CBP have made arrangements with foreign government entities to mutually recognize inspections of each other's ports and maritime supply chains through the IPS and Customs-Trade Partnership Against Terrorism (C-TPAT) programs. CBP has also utilized technological improvements to target some U.S.-bound cargo shipments remotely from the United States to reduce CSI staff in foreign countries. However, CBP faces political and legal constraints in host countries. For example, according to CBP and government officials in one country, a national law precludes the transmission of electronic scanned images other than to host government Customs officials. As a result, CSI officials must be present at each CSI port in that country to view the scanned images. Further, in some ports, CBP has made efforts to expand the scope of its CSI targeting to include contraband other than WMD, but that is subject to approval by the host governments.

ABBREVIATIONS

AEO	authorized economic operator
ATS	Automated Targeting System
CBP	U.S. Customs and Border Protection
CSI	Container Security Initiative
C-TPAT	Customs-Trade Partnership Against Terrorism
DHS	Department of Homeland Security
DOE	Department of Energy
IPS	International Port Security program
ISPS Code	International Ship and Port Facility Security Code

MOU	memorandum of understanding
MRA	mutual recognition arrangement
MTSA	Maritime Transportation Security Act
NTC-C	National Targeting Center-Cargo
SAFE Port Act	Security and Accountability for Every Port Act
WMD	weapons of mass destruction

* * *

September 16, 2013

The Honorable Thomas R. Carper
Chairman
The Honorable Tom Coburn
Ranking Member
Committee on Homeland Security and Governmental Affairs
United States Senate

The Honorable Susan M. Collins
United States Senate

Foreign ports and the cargo carried by vessels from these ports are critical to the U.S. economy but can also be exploited by terrorists. According to the U.S. Department of Transportation, the majority of U.S. imports arrive by ocean vessel, and much of that is transported in cargo containers.[1] Cargo containers are an important segment of the global supply chain—the flow of goods from manufacturers to retailers—and can present significant security concerns. For example, a 2012 risk assessment by the Department of Homeland Security (DHS) found that attacks could cause major disruptions to the maritime supply chain. DHS officials believe that the likelihood of terrorists smuggling weapons of mass destruction (WMD) into the United States in cargo containers is relatively low; however, the consequences of such an event could be catastrophic. Although there have been no known incidents of cargo containers being used to transport WMD, ensuring the security of cargo containers remains an important role for the federal government given that criminals have exploited containers for other illegal purposes, such as smuggling weapons, people, and illicit substances. To balance the government's need to help secure the global supply chain while also promoting the efficient and secure movement of goods, the White House issued the National Strategy for Global Supply Chain Security in January 2012, which emphasizes a risk-informed approach for DHS's cargo security programs across all modes of transportation.[2] This strategy builds on a number of strategic efforts to strengthen the global supply chain.[3] While DHS' cargo security programs cover all modes of transportation, the focus of this report is on DHS's maritime security programs.

In the federal government, U.S. Customs and Border Protection (CBP) and the Coast Guard, both within DHS, are two key agencies responsible for maritime security issues. In particular, CBP is responsible for, among other things, assessing the overall security of the supply chain and reducing the vulnerabilities associated with U.S.-bound cargo container shipments; and the Coast Guard is responsible for, among other things, assessing the effectiveness of security measures in foreign ports and vessels that trade with the United States.

In performing its container security responsibilities, CBP has developed a layered, risk management approach[4] that includes two security programs—the Container Security Initiative (CSI) and the Customs-Trade Partnership Against Terrorism (C-TPAT) program. Under the CSI program, CBP places officials (targeters) at select foreign seaports to use intelligence and risk assessment information to determine whether U.S.- bound cargo container shipments from those ports are at risk of containing WMD or other terrorist contraband. To aid in this process, CBP targeters use the Automated Targeting System (ATS)—an enforcement and decision support system that incorporates a set of rules to assess information provided by supply chain parties, such as importers—to identify high-risk shipments. C-TPAT is a voluntary program in which CBP officials work with private companies, referred to as partners, to review the security of their international supply chains and improve the security of their shipments to the United States. In return, C-TPAT partners receive various incentives to facilitate the flow of legitimate cargo, such as reduced scrutiny of their shipments.

In addition to the CBP container security programs, the Coast Guard operates the International Port Security (IPS) program in which Coast Guard officials, in conjunction with foreign officials, visit and assess the implementation of security measures in foreign ports against established, international port security standards to help ensure the security of maritime commerce. In addition, CBP and the Coast Guard have separately entered into arrangements with foreign counterpart agencies to validate and mutually recognize each others' port security practices to more efficiently address maritime and supply chain security.

Since September 11, 2001, Congress has passed various laws to address concerns about the security of maritime cargo container shipments in the global supply chain. The Maritime Transportation Security Act of 2002 (MTSA)[5] called for the establishment of a program to evaluate and certify secure systems of international transportation, including standards and procedures for screening and evaluating cargo containers prior to loading them onto vessels and for securing and monitoring cargo while in transit.[6] One MTSA provision requires DHS to assess the effectiveness of the antiterrorism measures maintained at ports from which foreign vessels depart to the United States, or in any other port the Secretary of Homeland Security believes may pose a risk to international maritime commerce.[7] The Secretary delegated this responsibility to the Coast Guard, which initiated IPS in 2004 to carry out this responsibility. To further address container security concerns, Congress passed, and the President signed, the Security and Accountability for Every (SAFE) Port Act in 2006, which included provisions that codified the CSI and C-TPAT programs.[8]

Given the importance of maritime transportation to the economy, the wide spectrum of security threats, and the constrained budget environment, you asked that we review DHS's maritime supply chain security programs. In particular, this report addresses the following questions:

- To what extent has DHS assessed the risks to the global supply chain associated with foreign ports and focused its maritime security programs to address those risks?
- What actions has DHS taken to help ensure the efficiency and effectiveness of its maritime supply chain security programs?

To address the first question, we identified how DHS's components assess risk to the supply chain associated with foreign ports and countries.[9] Specifically, we (1) gathered information on the criteria used to determine high-risk locations and the key stakeholders involved in developing any models or methodologies used to do so, (2) reviewed the methodology used to construct any models, and (3) determined the sufficiency of the models to identify high-risk locations. In particular, we reviewed the Coast Guard's IPS model for determining operational decisions, the methodology CBP used to select CSI ports, and the model developed by CBP and the Department of Energy (DOE) for potentially expanding cargo-scanning operations at foreign ports. To the extent possible, we compared the relative risk of foreign ports generated by these models with the location of CSI ports to determine the degree of correlation. As part of this process, we combined fiscal year 2012 data on the number of U.S.-bound shipments from foreign ports with data from the models and narrowed the list of ports based on a minimum of 1,000 U.S.-bound shipments—a step CBP took when developing its model in conjunction with DOE. We assessed the reliability of the models by interviewing staff responsible for development of the methodologies and the data and reviewing documentation related to the development, application, and reviews of the models. We concluded that the models and data were sufficiently reliable for the purposes of our review. In addition, we interviewed CBP, Coast Guard, DOE, and Department of State officials about the process used for identifying high-risk locations, the stakeholders involved in this process, and the status of these efforts. We compared this information with SAFE Port Act requirements, key elements for a risk management approach,[10] and the principles laid out in the *National Strategy for Global Supply Chain Security*. We also reviewed our prior work on risk management practices and compared our analysis of CBP's actions with those practices.[11]

To address the second question, we focused primarily on the CSI, CTPAT, and IPS programs. Specifically, we analyzed CBP efforts to implement the fiscal year 2012 through 2017 CBP Office of Field Operations Strategic Plan and associated strategies in the CSI and CTPAT Strategy Action Plans. We reviewed DHS documentation, such as the 2013 *DHS Annual Performance Report* and budget documents. Further, we reviewed CSI and C-TPAT performance measurement data and analyzed CSI staffing data from fiscal years 2009 through fiscal years 2012—the 4 most recent years for which data were available—to review the extent to which CSI staffing models have increased efficiency.

In addition, we analyzed fiscal year 2012 Coast Guard foreign port visit data and foreign country risk data to determine the extent to which the Coast Guard uses the results of its risk assessments to help determine the amount of resources needed when visiting foreign countries' ports.

We reviewed documentation related to the data sources, such as the 2013 *DHS Annual Performance Report*, and obtained written responses from knowledgeable agency officials regarding any issues with completeness, accuracy, and management of the data. We determined that these CBP and Coast Guard data were sufficiently reliable for the purposes of our review. We visited six geographically dispersed foreign countries that participate in the CSI program—two each in Latin America (Panama and Argentina), Asia (Japan and Singapore), and Europe (the Netherlands and England)—that also provided a range of coverage regarding (1) cargo container shipment risk levels, (2) volume of cargo containers shipped to the United States, (3) the proportion of transshipped containers,[12] and (4) participation in mutual recognition arrangements (MRA) with CBP or the Coast Guard.[13] We interviewed DHS, Department of State, and foreign government officials in the countries we visited, and also met with other maritime supply chain stakeholders, such as officials from private industry and the World Customs Organization, to discuss implementation of DHS's maritime security programs, how these programs are integrated, the specific maritime security threats each program targets, and the impact of these programs on the security of U.S.-bound cargo container shipments. We worked with relevant officials at the U.S. embassies in the foreign countries we visited to help us determine which foreign government and industry officials to interview. The results from our visits to these six countries cannot be generalized; however, the visits provided us with first-hand observations on cargo security screening and targeting practices at the ports visited, and insights regarding how DHS implements its overseas maritime container security programs and the impact of these programs.

In addition, we contacted officials from the seven partners that have signed an MRA with CBP and obtained the views of cognizant officials representing four of these partners. While the results of these meetings cannot be generalized to all seven MRA-signatory partners, they provided insights regarding the impact of the MRAs on DHS and other maritime security programs.

Further, we interviewed the DHS Acting Director of Transportation & Cargo, Transborder Policy, to discuss implementation of the *National Strategy for Global Supply Chain Security* and how it affects maritime container security programs. We also interviewed Coast Guard officials responsible for the IPS program to discuss development and implementation of the Coast Guard IPS risk model and mutual recognition efforts.[14]

We conducted this performance audit from October 2012 to September 2013 in accordance with generally accepted government auditing standards. Those standards require that we plan and perform the audit to obtain sufficient, appropriate evidence to provide a reasonable basis for our findings and conclusions based on our audit objectives. We believe that the evidence obtained provides a reasonable basis for our findings and conclusions based on our audit objectives.

BACKGROUND

Vulnerabilities of Maritime Cargo Containers in the Global Supply Chain

Ports are critical gateways for the movement of commerce through the global supply chain. According to CBP data, in fiscal year 2012, about 11.5 million cargo container shipments arrived from more than 650 foreign ports—meaning roughly 31,000 maritime container shipments arrived each day that year. The facilities, vessels, and infrastructure within ports, and the cargo passing through them, all have vulnerabilities that terrorists could exploit. Every time responsibility for cargo in containers changes hands along the supply chain there is the potential for a security breach. While there have been no known incidents of containers being used to transport WMDs, criminals have exploited containers for other illegal purposes, such as smuggling weapons, people, and illicit substances. Figure 1 illustrates the notional key points of transfer involved in the global supply chain—from the time that a container is loaded with goods at a foreign factory to its arrival at the U.S. seaport and ultimately the U.S. importer.

DHS Efforts to Secure the Global Supply Chain

DHS has taken steps to secure the global supply chain, including the cargo in oceangoing containers destined for the United States. DHS's strategy includes focusing security efforts beyond U.S. borders to target and examine high-risk cargo and vessels before they enter U.S. seaports. DHS's strategy is based on a layered approach of related programs that attempt to focus resources on potentially risky foreign ports, vessels, and cargo container shipments while allowing other cargo container shipments to proceed without unduly disrupting the flow of commerce into the United States. DHS's maritime security programs support the *National Strategy for Global Supply Chain Security*, which emphasizes risk management and coordinated engagement with key stakeholders who also have supply chain roles and responsibilities. Figure 2 shows DHS's key maritime security programs and the various segments in the global supply chain where these programs are focused.

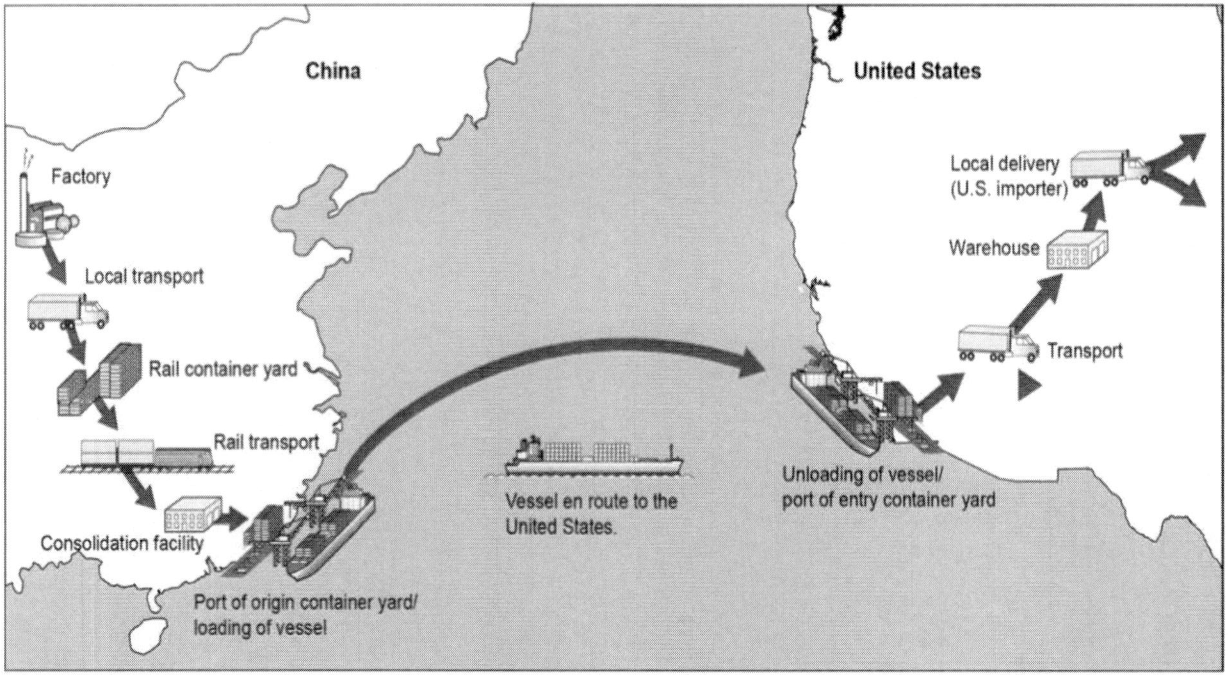

Source: GAO; Map Resources (map).

Figure 1. Illustrative Example of Key Points in the Global Supply Chain.

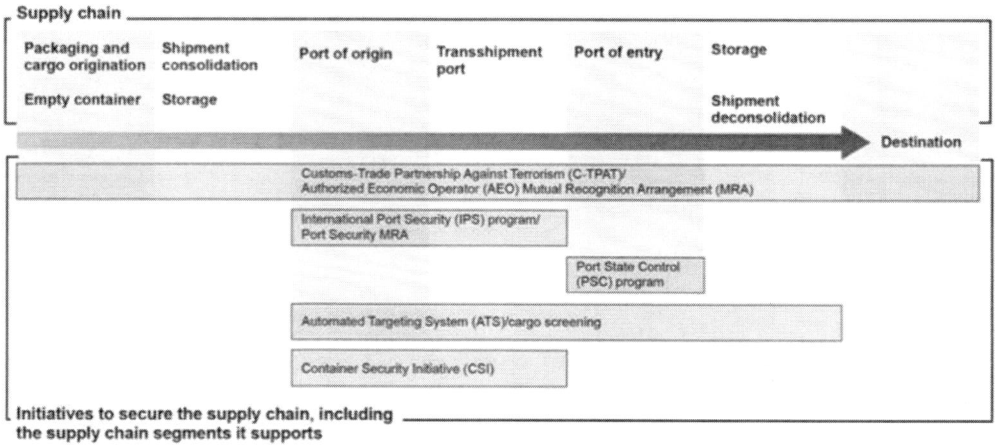

Program and year introduced	Responsible DHS component	Description
Container Security Initiative, 2002	CBP	Customs and Border Protection (CBP), through the CSI program, places staff at participating foreign seaports to work with host country customs officials to identify and examine high-risk cargo containers for weapons of mass destruction before they are shipped to the United States. CBP officials identify the high-risk containers and request that their foreign counterparts examine the contents of the containers. For the CSI program, CBP officials stated that DHS expended about $56.7 million in fiscal year 2012.
Customs-Trade Partnership Against Terrorism, 2001	CBP	CBP develops voluntary partnerships with members of the international trade community composed of importers; customs brokers; forwarders; air, sea, and land carriers; contract logistics providers; and marine port terminals. Private companies agree to improve the security of their supply chains in return for various benefits, such as a reduced likelihood that their containers will be examined. CBP officials stated that DHS expended about $37.2 million for C-TPAT in fiscal year 2012.
International Port Security program, 2004	Coast Guard	Under the IPS program, the Coast Guard visits foreign ports to assess compliance with international security standards. For fiscal year 2012, Coast Guard officials reported that the IPS program had an annual operating budget of about $3.3 million.
Port State Control program, 2004	Coast Guard	In the PSC, the Coast Guard uses risk-based criteria to identify which foreign vessels entering U.S. ports it considers to be at risk of noncompliance with international and domestic regulations, and performs compliance examinations of these vessels.

Source: GAO analysis of information provided by DHS.

Notes: AEOs include, for example, manufacturers, importers, exporters, brokers, ports, airports, terminal operators, warehouses, and distributors.

Through MRAs with other partners, the security-related practices and programs taken by the Customs or maritime security administration of one country are recognized and accepted by the administration of another.

ATS is a CBP enforcement and decision support system that incorporates a set of rules to assess information provided by supply chain parties, such as importers, to identify high risk shipments.

Figure 2. Department of Homeland Security's (DHS) Key Maritime Security Programs.

Container Security Initiative

CSI is a program that aims to identify and examine U.S.-bound cargo container shipments that could pose a high risk of concealing WMDs or other terrorist contraband by reviewing advanced cargo information about the shipments. As part of the CSI program, CBP officers are stationed at select foreign seaports to identify high-risk U.S.-bound container cargo shipments before they are loaded onto U.S.-bound vessels. As of July 2013, there were 58 CSI ports in 32 countries that, collectively, account for over 80 percent of the container shipments imported into the United States. In addition to the CSI ports where CBP placed targeters, CBP also entered into arrangements with Australia and New Zealand to remotely target U.S.-bound cargo container shipments from the United States.[15] A complete listing of the countries that participate in the CSI program can be found in appendix I.

CBP officers stationed at foreign CSI ports are to conduct the following activities:

- **Target U.S.-bound container shipments**. As we previously reported, CBP targeters use ATS and other information to electronically review information about U.S.-bound shipments departing from the foreign port—a process CBP refers to as screening.[16] CBP targeters review the ATS risk scores and additional information to identify high-risk shipments with a potential nexus to terrorism—a process referred to as targeting. The CBP targeters make a final determination about which containers are high risk and will be referred to host government officials for examination.
- **Request examinations of high-risk container shipments**. According to our work and updates provided by CBP officials, CBP targeters work with host country government officials to mitigate high-risk container shipments.[17] Actions may include resolving discrepancies in shipment information, scanning cargo containers' contents with radiation detection or imaging equipment (as shown in fig. 3), or conducting physical inspections of the containers' contents.

Customs-Trade Partnership against Terrorism

According to our prior work and updates provided by CBP officials, C-TPAT aims to secure the flow of goods bound for the United States by developing a voluntary public-private sector partnership with stakeholders of the international trade community.[18] C-TPAT partners agree to adhere to the program's eight established minimum security criteria in areas such as physical security, personnel security, and information technology. CTPAT partners also agree to provide CBP with information regarding their security processes and procedures and allow CBP to validate or verify that these security measures are in place. In return, C-TPAT partners receive various incentives, such as reduced examinations based upon lower risk scores.

Source: GAO.

Figure 3. Panama Customs Examining a Container Using Imaging Equipment, Port of Balboa, Panama.

International Port Security Program

In addition to the CBP programs, the Coast Guard also has an internationally focused maritime security program, the IPS program. Under the IPS program, Coast Guard officials visit foreign ports to evaluate their antiterrorism security measures against established International Ship and Port Facility Security (ISPS) Code standards.[19] In addition, the Coast Guard collects and shares best practices with foreign countries and engages in efforts to help facilitate a comprehensive and consistent approach to maritime security in ports worldwide. Coast Guard officials reported that from its inception in April 2004 through June 2013, IPS program officials have visited port facilities in 151 countries and overseas protectorates engaged in maritime trade with the United States. According to its visits and the information provided by the foreign countries as part of those visits, the Coast Guard determines whether the countries have effectively implemented the ISPS Code and are maintaining effective security measures in their ports. If the Coast Guard finds that a country is not maintaining port security measures, the Coast Guard can impose conditions of entry on vessels arriving at the United States from that country.[20]

Port State Control Program

The Coast Guard uses the results of the port risk assessments to help decide which foreign vessels to board or inspect through its Port State Control program, according to the U.S. Coast Guard *International Port Security Program: Annual Report 2012*.[21] While the Port State Control program does not directly affect container security, as part of this program, the Coast Guard uses risk-based criteria to identify which foreign vessels entering U.S. ports and waterways it considers to be at risk of noncompliance with international or domestic regulations, and performs compliance examinations of these vessels. The risk-based criteria include the vessel's management, the flag state that the vessel is registered under, the vessel's recognized security organization, and the vessel's security compliance history resulting from previous examinations.

Mutual Recognition Arrangements

Through mutual recognition arrangements with foreign partners, the security-related practices and programs taken by the Customs or maritime security administration of one partner are recognized and accepted by the administration of another.[22] Both CBP and the Coast Guard have entered into such arrangements. For example, CBP can expand the reach of its supply chain security programs through MRAs. According to the World Customs Organization, mutual recognition allows Customs administrations to target high-risk shipments more effectively and expedite low-risk shipments by, for example, reducing redundant examinations.[23] The World Customs Organization distinguishes between mutual recognition of Customs controls and mutual recognition of authorized economic operator (AEO) programs:[24]

- **Mutual recognition of Customs controls (Customs-to-Customs MRAs):** This is achieved when, for example, the Customs administrations of two countries have confidence in and accept each other's procedures for targeting and inspecting cargo shipped in containers.

- **Mutual recognition of AEO programs (AEO MRAs):** This occurs when Customs administrations agree to recognize one another's AEO programs and security features and to provide comparable benefits to members of the respective programs.

In the United States, C-TPAT is the designated AEO program and businesses participating in the program are AEOs. According to C-TPAT documentation, CBP has developed an AEO MRA process involving four phases: (1) a comparison of the program requirements to determine if the programs align on basic principles; (2) a pilot program of joint validation visits to determine if the programs align in basic practice; (3) the signing of an MRA; and (4) the development of mutual recognition operational procedures, primarily those associated with information sharing. MRAs are based on close working relationships between Customs administrations, which allow for the exchange of information, intelligence, and documents in an effort to assist countries in the prevention and investigation of Customs offenses.

The Coast Guard can also enter into MRAs that recognize international maritime security practices of other foreign governments. For example, the Coast Guard has a process in place to recognize the port inspection procedures of other countries.

One Hundred Percent Scanning Requirement

Although DHS's maritime security programs support the National Strategy for Global Supply Chain Security and the strategy's risk-informed security approach, the SAFE Port Act included requirements that pilot projects be established to test the feasibility of scanning 100 percent of U.S.-bound cargo containers at foreign ports.[25] Subsequently, the Implementing Recommendations of the 9/11 Commission Act of 2007 (9/11 Act) required, among other things, that by July 2012, 100 percent of U.S.- bound cargo containers be scanned at foreign ports with both radiation detection and nonintrusive inspection (imaging) equipment before being placed onto U.S.-bound vessels.[26]

In June 2008 and in October 2009, we found that CBP faced numerous challenges in implementing the 100 percent scanning requirement at the pilot ports.[27] In October 2009, we recommended, among other things, that CBP conduct feasibility and cost-benefit analyses of implementing the 100 percent scanning requirement and provide the results to Congress along with any suggestions of cost-effective alternatives to implementing the 100 percent scanning requirement, as appropriate. CBP partially concurred with the recommendations but did not implement them. According to CBP officials, CBP does not plan to conduct these analyses related to achieving the 100 percent scanning requirement because the pilot project has been reduced in scope and currently there are no funds to conduct such analyses. In February 2012, we reported that the scanning challenges continued, and CBP achieved 100 percent scanning of U.S.-bound cargo containers at only one foreign pilot port where it was being attempted—Port Qasim, Pakistan.[28] In May 2012, the Secretary of Homeland Security announced a 2-year extension of the deadline—until July 2014—for implementing the requirement that cargo containers not enter the United States unless they are scanned at foreign ports prior to being loaded on vessels.[29] In its report to Congress that same month, DHS stated that it recognizes the need to proceed with its container security programs in a manner that maximizes the security of maritime cargo and facilitates its movement. DHS added that it plans to continue working with other federal agencies and international partners to develop technology and enhance risk management processes, in addition to continuing its existing container security programs.[30] According to the January 2013 *National Strategy for Global Supply Chain Security Implementation Update*, DHS is working to identify potential alternatives to 100 percent scanning, and a senior DHS official told us that DHS's layered security strategy will be a key component of the alternative.[31]

DHS Has Developed Models to Assess Foreign Port Risks, but CBP Has Not Assessed Whether Its CSI Locations Remain Valid

The Coast Guard and CBP, DHS components with maritime security responsibilities, have developed models to assess the risks of foreign ports and the cargo carried by vessels from these ports. The Coast Guard uses the model it developed to inform operational decisions for its IPS program and updates its assessment annually. In contrast, in 2009, CBP developed a risk model to begin the process of expanding its efforts to scan 100 percent of U.S.-bound container shipments, but the model was never implemented. As a result, it does not know whether the ports included in CSI remain valid.

The Coast Guard Has Developed a Model to Regularly Assess Risks of Foreign Ports and Inform Operational Decisions

The Coast Guard has developed a risk-informed model as part of its IPS program to regularly assess the potential threat foreign ports pose to the maritime supply chain and make operational decisions regarding foreign ports' security measures. According to the 2012 IPS program annual report, this risk model includes four components, summarized below, that help the Coast Guard focus IPS program resources.

Country Threat

The Coast Guard uses security and commerce data as well as measures on government decision making, such as the prevalence of corruption, to assess the likelihood of terrorists using a foreign port to import WMDs or other contraband into the United States. In particular, the Coast Guard relies on CBP trade information, the U.S. Department of State's Security Environment Threat List, World Bank reports, and other data to determine whether countries represent a normal, medium, or high security risk.

Foreign Port Assessment

MTSA, as amended by the SAFE Port Act, requires the Coast Guard to reassess countries' ports every 3 years, and during these visits, IPS officials use two data checklists, one that assesses government performance and one that assesses facilities' performance.[32] The government performance checklist measures how well a government gathers and assesses information on security threats, and reviews and approves port facility security plans, among other things. The facilities performance checklist measures port security measures implemented to prevent unauthorized cargo and people from entering the port. Such security measures include, for example, perimeter security and access procedures for port facility employees and visitors.

Country Responsiveness

The IPS model includes measures of the political, economic, and social conditions in a country to help determine whether countries are likely to efficiently utilize Coast Guard assistance. The model incorporates information on corruption, inflation, and "people measures," such as infant mortality rates and literacy rates.

Country Wealth

The IPS model includes a measure of national income to determine if the country can afford to maintain security measures on its own or whether it is likely to require foreign assistance.

According to the 2012 IPS program annual report, the Coast Guard combines these components into a single risk model and uses the results to make informed decisions on how to engage each country with the IPS program, including (1) how often to visit ports, (2) how many staff to assign to a particular visit, and (3) whether the country requires assistance. Specifically, the Coast Guard visits foreign ports in higher-risk countries more frequently (and with more IPS officials) than in ports in lower-risk countries, which we discuss later in this report. In addition, the IPS annual report states that the Coast Guard uses the country threat component of the IPS risk model to help determine which foreign vessels to board as part of its Port State Control program. The Coast Guard updates its risk model annually. While elements of the Coast Guard's risk model could be used to inform maritime container security efforts, there are limits regarding how it can be applied to maritime supply chain security because the IPS program is focused on assessing port security. Unlike the CBP risk model described below, the Coast Guard's model is not designed to assess the risk of maritime cargo shipments imported from foreign ports (e.g., transshipped cargo).

CBP Considered Risk in Establishing Some CSI Ports, but Has Not Assessed Whether CSI Currently Covers the Riskiest Ports

CBP Selected Initial CSI Ports Largely on the Basis of Volume and Used More Risk Factors when Expanding CSI Locations

In 2002, CBP selected the initial 23 CSI ports largely on the basis of the volume of U.S.-bound container cargo, but increased the number of risk factors in selecting additional ports as it expanded the CSI program beginning in 2003.[33] Specifically, according to CBP documentation, volume was a key criterion for assessing which foreign ports represented the greatest threat to the United States. Figure 4 shows the large number of containers shipped through the Port of Singapore, one of the original CSI ports.

Source: GAO.

Figure 4. Partial View of the Port of Singapore.

After selecting these initial 23 ports, CBP subsequently added 35 ports to the CSI program from 2003 through 2007 on the basis of additional criteria, such as strategic threat factors and diplomatic or political considerations. Through these expansion efforts, in 2007 CBP reached its goal of staffing 58 CSI ports that, collectively, cover over 80 percent of U.S.-bound container shipments.[34] We reported in 2008 that CBP did not have plans to add other ports to the CSI program because, according to CBP, the costs associated with expanding the program would outweigh the potential benefits.[35]

CBP Developed a Risk Model for Expanding Container Security Efforts at High-Risk Ports, but It Was Never Implemented

In 2009, CBP developed a risk model in conjunction with DOE to begin the process of expanding its efforts to scan 100 percent of U.S.-bound container shipments for a related program, but the model was never implemented. In particular, in April 2009, the Secretary of Homeland Security approved the "strategic trade corridor strategy" as an approach to expanding CBP's efforts to scan U.S.-bound container cargo beyond the original pilot locations.[36] As part of this expansion effort, CBP developed a model—assisted by DOE—to rank potential foreign ports on the basis of risks associated with countries and maritime commerce, as well as the number and percentage of high-risk, U.S.-bound shipments processed. Specifically, DOE provided the country threat and shipping lane information from the model it used to identify and prioritize foreign ports for participation in the Megaports Initiative,[37] and CBP provided the high-risk shipment data from ATS. CBP and DOE completed their initial analyses in February 2009, which identified 356 potential expansion ports ranked by risk, and CBP narrowed the list down to 187 ports by considering only ports that had at least 1,000 shipments per year to the United States. CBP collaborated with DOE, the Department of State, and the intelligence community to prioritize 22 ports for expansion of 100 percent scanning efforts on the basis of such factors as the model's risk ranking and the volume of U.S.-bound cargo container shipments. CBP ultimately did not pursue this strategy, given cargo security program budget cuts and the Secretary of Homeland Security's decision to extend the deadline for 100 percent scanning until July 2014.

The results of the 2009 strategic trade corridor prioritization model show that the CSI program is operating at some of the riskiest foreign ports, but it also operates at ports that are less risky. Since the model focused on U.S.-bound maritime containerized cargo, its results could be used as a proxy measure to assess whether CSI ports coincide with those foreign locations that pose the greatest risk to the global supply chain. We combined the risk rankings for the 356 ports in the 2009 model with fiscal year 2012 U.S.-bound shipment data and excluded ports with fewer than 1,000 U.S.-bound shipments per year, which narrowed the list to 138 ports.[38] Comparing the CSI ports with the results shows that CSI did not have a presence at about half of the ports CBP considered higher risk, and about one-fifth of the existing CSI ports were at lower-risk locations. Specifically, of the 61 current CSI ports, 57 had at least 1,000 U.S.-bound shipments in fiscal year 2012. Of these 57 CSI ports, 27 were within the top 50 riskiest ports, 18 ports were between the 51st and 100th riskiest ports, and 12 ports were not among the top 100 riskiest ports. Of the remaining 4 CSI ports, 3 had fewer than 1,000 U.S.-bound shipments and 1 port was not ranked in the 2009 risk model. According to CBP officials, CBP has not established CSI locations in 15 of the top 50 riskiest ports either because host governments have not been cooperative regarding CBP cargo examination requests or CBP was not able to negotiate an arrangement with host governments to establish CSI operations, as discussed below.

CBP officials stated that factors have changed since the model was developed in 2009, and they do not consider all of the same ports to be high risk at this time. For example, one potential expansion port the model classified as higher risk in 2009 now ships fewer containers to the United States, and CBP officials reported that they would not currently consider including this port in the CSI program. Further, according to CBP's fiscal year 2012 budget submission, CBP considered closing several CSI ports while maintaining CSI operations in strategically important ports. Given this information, and the fact that the number and location of CSI ports has generally not changed since 2009, the CSI program's current locations may not be in alignment with the highest-risk ports. Because the CSI program depends on the willingness of sovereign host countries to participate in the program, there are challenges to implementing CSI and CBP efforts to negotiate with other countries to expand the CSI program, and these efforts have not always been successful. CBP and the Department of State point to challenges in implementing CSI in high-risk countries, such as CBP officer safety, funding concerns, and the willingness of host country governments to facilitate requested cargo examinations of U.S.-bound shipments. CBP officials stated that CBP is not pursuing the strategic trade corridor strategy, but they noted that since the beginning of the CSI program, CBP has made efforts to negotiate to establish CSI ports within four countries that have ports representing potential significant risks. These efforts were not successful in three countries for political reasons. For example, the legislature in one of these countries did not approve the placement of CSI in its country. However, according to CBP officials, CBP has signed a declaration of principles to place CSI in an additional foreign country and estimates that CSI will be operational within this country by the end of fiscal year 2014.

CBP Has Not Assessed the Risks of Foreign Ports that Ship Cargo to the United States since 2005

CBP has not assessed the risk of foreign ports that ship cargo to the United States for its CSI program since completing the CSI expansion analysis in 2005. CBP officials stated they have not performed any such risk assessments since 2005 because CBP does not have any specific expansion plans for the CSI program. However, our work indicates that CBP may expand CSI. In particular, CBP's fiscal year 2013 and 2014 budget requests noted that CBP may expand CSI in the future to additional countries of strategic interest, if feasible; and CBP officials told us that CBP is finalizing negotiations with a foreign government to expand CSI to an additional port, as discussed above.

We acknowledge that CBP may face challenges in including foreign ports that ship the riskiest cargo to the United States in its CSI program, but expanding CSI without assessing the security risk posed by foreign ports is contrary to agency policy. In particular, according to the CSI Statement of Policy and Intent signed by the CBP Commissioner in April 2011, CBP is to prioritize CSI expansion locations in accordance with the *National Strategy for Global Supply Chain Security*, which states that the federal government should take a risk-informed approach to secure the global supply chain. Further, the SAFE Port Act provides that DHS/CBP is to assess the costs, benefits, and other factors associated with designation of a CSI port, including the level of risk for the potential compromise of containers by terrorists, or other threats as determined by DHS; the volume of cargo being imported to the United States directly from, or being transshipped through, the foreign seaport; and the results of the Coast Guard's IPS assessments.[39]

In addition to not completing a risk assessment to help inform potential CSI expansion, CBP has also not assessed the risk of its current CSI ports—some of which have participated in CSI for more than a decade— to determine if they remain valid on the basis of risk. CBP officials stated that they have not conducted such an assessment because a couple of factors make it difficult to close CSI ports and reallocate resources to prospective new CSI ports. In particular, the officials stated that (1) removing CSI from a country might negatively affect political relations with the host government, and (2) uncertain CSI funding in future years could make it difficult for CBP to make plans to close lower-risk CSI ports and open new CSI ports at higher-risk locations. Specifically, CBP officials estimate that it could take about 1 year to close a CSI port and 2 years or more to open a new port, and, given budget uncertainties, CBP has not pursued such efforts.

It is unclear if the political and cost challenges CBP officials identified would affect any reallocation of CSI resources to prospective new CSI ports, but these challenges do not preclude CBP from assessing the risk of its current CSI locations. Regarding the impact of changes to the CSI program on political relations, CBP officials stated they routinely speak to host government officials during CSI evaluations about how to strengthen the program, but these officials said that the discussions have not specifically included the impact on relations with the host government of removing lower-risk ports from the CSI program. Further, it is unclear if reallocating resources from current CSI ports to higher-risk ports would ultimately increase costs because some costs—such as staffing costs and office space leases—could be lower in some of the new locations than costs in the lower-risk ports it would be leaving. Moreover, the DHS *National Infrastructure Protection Plan*[40] and our *Risk Management Framework*[41] state that risk assessments, the effectiveness of measures to deal with risks, and the costs of those measures are to inform decisions. Our framework also states that agencies should periodically evaluate the cost-effectiveness of their programs and that mechanisms for altering a program should be in place based on current risk data. In addition, the DHS *National Infrastructure Protection Plan* states that effective protective programs seek to use resources efficiently by focusing on actions that offer the greatest mitigation of risk for any given expenditure. The plan also states that risk management includes a feedback loop that continually incorporates new information, such as changing threats or the effect of actions taken to reduce or eliminate identified threats, vulnerabilities, or consequences. We recognize that it may not be possible to include all the higher-risk ports in CSI because CSI requires the cooperation of sovereign foreign governments and because of concerns regarding the security of U.S. personnel that may be staffed in those countries. Nevertheless, given that CBP is no longer pursuing implementation of 100 percent scanning, it is important that CBP apply the risk management principles discussed above to CSI—a risk-informed program—to more effectively mitigate the threat of high-risk cargo before it is shipped to the United States. Periodically assessing the risk level of cargo shipped from foreign ports and using the results of these risk assessments to inform the CSI locations would help ensure that CBP is allocating its resources to provide the greatest possible coverage of high-risk cargo to best mitigate the risk of importing WMDs or other terrorist contraband into the United States through the maritime supply chain.

DHS Has Taken Steps to Improve the Efficiency and Effectiveness of Its Maritime Container Security Programs, but Faces Constraints

DHS, through the Coast Guard and CBP, has taken a number of steps to improve the efficiency and effectiveness of its maritime security programs to reduce global supply chain risks. In this regard, the Coast Guard's actions have primarily been focused on the IPS program. CBP has continued its efforts to expand or refine its C-TPAT and CSI programs, but faces host country political and legal constraints.

The Coast Guard Has Worked to Reduce Global Supply Chain Risks by More Efficiently and Effectively Using IPS Resources

The Coast Guard has worked to use resources more effectively and reduce risks at foreign ports and from U.S.-bound vessels through its IPS program by implementing a risk-informed model that prioritizes the countries to visit and provide with assistance. When the Coast Guard first implemented the IPS program in 2004, it was required by MTSA to assess the effectiveness of antiterrorism measures maintained in ports where U.S. vessels call or from which vessels depart for the United States. As a result, the Coast Guard focused on completing initial visits of foreign ports to determine ISPS Code compliance, but did not have a methodology to prioritize follow-up visits and help countries increase their level of port security. To accomplish these goals, in 2005, the Coast Guard began developing its IPS risk model to assess the risks of foreign ports and prioritize assistance, which it fully integrated into IPS operations in 2011. The Coast Guard classifies countries as normal, medium, or high security risks and completes port security checklists during foreign port visits.

The Coast Guard Uses Its Risk Assessments to Manage Port Visits and Allocate Foreign Assistance

According to the 2012 IPS program annual report, the Coast Guard uses the results of its risk assessments to help determine the amount of resources needed to visit foreign countries' ports, board foreign vessels, and track port security improvements. Specifically, the Coast Guard uses the risk model results to more efficiently and effectively allocate resources to help ensure that visits to foreign ports in higher-risk countries occur more frequently (and with more IPS officials) than to ports in lower-risk countries.[42] Table 1 provides information on Coast Guard IPS program visits, by country risk level, for fiscal year 2012.

Table 1. Coast Guard International Port Security Program Visits, by Country Risk Level, for Fiscal Year 2012

Foreign country risk level	Number of foreign countries visited[a]	Average number of staff days per visit[b]	Average cost per visit[c]
Normal risk	13	14	$9,926
Medium risk	18	29	$27,193
High risk	23	37	$38,214

Source: GAO analysis of Coast Guard data.

[a]Through the International Port Security program, the Coast Guard makes a determination of country, not port, risk level.

[b]Staff days are cumulative for all Coast Guard staff involved in foreign port visits. According to Coast Guard officials, many visits were the result of multiple trips and often included different staff on the team.

[c]According to Coast Guard officials, costs reflect travel and per diem costs as well as any funds provided to the U.S. embassy for translators, additional security, and in-country flights, among other things. They do not reflect any salary or overhead costs.

IPS program officials we met with that are responsible for assessing ports in Africa and Southeast Asia stated that this risk-informed approach helps the Coast Guard more efficiently use its resources. Further, the IPS program has enabled the Coast Guard to measure foreign countries' port security based on improvements its officials observe when completing foreign port visits. According to the 2012 IPS program annual report, port assessment scores have improved worldwide since the Coast Guard initiated the IPS program in 2004. The Coast Guard attributes this success, in part, to implementation of the IPS risk model.

According to the 2012 IPS program annual report, the Coast Guard also uses the results of the IPS model to allocate foreign assistance. The risk model includes (1) country threat information; (2) port visit results; (3) a determination of which countries are most likely to benefit from assistance to improve port security, such as port security training; and (4) the individual country's ability to best use assistance funds and sustain security efforts, as discussed earlier in this report. The 2012 report also states that Coast Guard officials are to use this information to direct resources to those foreign countries where they believe the return on investment will be greatest. Further, this report states that the Coast Guard uses the results of the IPS risk model to help determine which foreign vessels to board as part of its Port State Control program. The risk-based screening tool the Coast Guard uses to select vessels to board assigns point values to various risk factors, such as country threat data from the IPS risk model. In addition, the Coast Guard boards foreign vessels that have recently stopped in higher-risk ports (i.e., countries that have not substantially implemented the ISPS Code).

MRAs May Allow the Coast Guard to Allocate Resources More Efficiently

In addition to prioritizing resources through its IPS risk model, the Coast Guard has worked with foreign governments to mutually recognize each other's maritime security programs, which can more efficiently use IPS resources and reduce risks. For example, in September 2012, the Coast Guard signed a memorandum of understanding (MOU) with the European Union that establishes a process for mutually recognizing security inspections of each other's ports.[43] The European Union has developed regulations for the consistent implementation of the ISPS Code by its member states and established a process for verifying the effectiveness of its member states' maritime security measures. This process includes European Union inspections of member states' ports that result in reports that (1) identify any nonconformities with the regulations and (2) make recommendations to address any nonconformities.

Under the MOU procedures, the Coast Guard recognizes a successful European Union inspection of its member states' ports in the same manner as it would recognize a successful country visit by Coast Guard IPS inspectors. Coast Guard IPS officials stated that they have collaborated with their European counterparts to develop standard operating procedures for these port inspections and they were used in a recent joint inspection of a container facility in Felixstowe, the United Kingdom. According to DHS documents and Coast Guard IPS officials in Europe, by signing this MOU, the Coast Guard plans to reassign some IPS officials from Europe to Africa, where certain countries are having more difficulties in implementing effective antiterrorism measures in their ports. Coast Guard IPS officials reported, however, that a trade-off of signing the MOU is that its IPS officials will not have the same opportunities to have face-to-face interactions and share port security information and practices directly with their European Union counterparts as in the past. Despite this trade-off, the Coast Guard IPS officials stated that entering into such arrangements increases efficiencies and noted that they intend to negotiate additional MOUs with other foreign governments that have strong port inspection programs.

CBP Has Worked to More Efficiently Use Resources and Expand Its C-TPAT Membership

CBP Has Taken Steps to More Efficiently Use Resources by Negotiating MRAs

CBP has worked with foreign partners to mutually recognize each other's AEO programs to more efficiently use resources while continuing to reduce risks to the global supply chain. According to the World Customs Organization, as of June 2013, there were 25 AEO programs worldwide, other than C-TPAT, with which CBP could enter into an MRA. As part of the evaluation of a foreign partner's capacity for entering into an MRA, CBP conducts joint validations with the other partner to ensure that a partner's AEO program has security standards that are equivalent to those required by the C-TPAT program. CBP officials stated that CBP does not pursue mutual recognition with a Customs administration that does not have an equivalent AEO program in place because doing so could compromise the security of U.S.-bound container shipments. As of July 2013, CBP had signed MRAs with seven foreign Customs administrations—New Zealand in 2007, Canada and Jordan in 2008, Japan in 2009, the Republic of (South) Korea in 2010, and the European Union and the Taipei Economic and Cultural Representative Office (Taiwan) in 2012—and is in the process of negotiating MRAs with five other partners. CBP officials stated that they expect to complete MRA negotiations with one partner by the end of fiscal year 2013 and that they generally complete one or two MRAs each year.

To help foreign countries establish AEO programs, CBP officials stated that the C-TPAT program provides training and technical assistance for foreign Customs agencies that request technical assistance. As of April 2013, CBP officials reported that C-TPAT has provided assistance to about 70 foreign countries and noted that this assistance improves global supply chain security. Further, CBP officials told us that the goal of this assistance is to establish AEO-MRAs with foreign Customs agencies as a means to increase efficiencies in supply chain security efforts. According to CBP officials, by relying on MRA partners to validate supply chain security procedures overseas, CBP is able to operate more efficiently by reducing the costs associated with conducting security validations. For example, in 2010, CBP completed a study on AEO validation visits conducted on its behalf in Japan and Canada by the respective host governments. On the basis of cost data from prior validation visits, CBP estimates the C-TPAT program saved over $290,000 and over 1,500 staff hours by accepting the 90 validations completed by the Japanese and Canadian governments during 2009 and 2010.[44] Further, according to CBP officials, mutual recognition leads to a common understanding of global supply chain security standards, resulting in greater program efficiency and a streamlined validation process by reducing the number of redundant validations. As a result, mutual recognition enables CBP to focus its resources on higher-risk supply chains. CBP officials also stated that AEO program officials are in a better position to conduct validations of companies within their respective AEO programs because these officials are proficient in the local language and are more familiar with the companies' supply chains.

MRAs can increase efficiencies in the C-TPAT program, but CBP faces challenges in implementing MRAs. According to C-TPAT data, since 2009, CBP has accepted over 480 validations conducted by staff from foreign governments that have signed MRAs with the United States. Further, these data show that the number of validations conducted by MRA partners has increased significantly each year from 2009 (26) through 2012 (285), and CBP officials stated that they expect the number of validations to continue to increase because the European Union and Taiwan—two of the United States' largest trading partners—are expected to conduct more validations in 2013. While MRAs have resulted in increased efficiencies, CBP and foreign government officials we met with identified challenges in implementing MRAs. For example, CBP and foreign government officials we met with stated that exchanging data across information technology systems can be difficult, and government officials from one foreign partner stated that differences in privacy laws between partners can create additional hurdles to information sharing. As a result, it may take time for the benefits to be evident to the AEO partners. Specifically, private sector trade officials in one country we visited reported that they had not yet realized the benefits of the MRA through reduced inspections of their shipments at U.S. ports. In addition, World Customs Organization officials we met with said that it may be difficult to document the benefits of MRAs through reduced inspections because U.S. agencies other than CBP also have their own inspection procedures for imported cargo that are not part of any MRA. For example, according to CBP, the Food and Drug Administration has its own inspection process. As a result, MRA participants' shipments could still be slowed. According to CBP officials, CBP is working with other federal agencies to harmonize the inspection process at ports of entry and accelerate inspection decision making to address this issue.

CBP has entered into AEO-MRAs with other partners, but does not have plans to negotiate Customs-to-Customs MRAs. Under a Customs-toCustoms MRA, joint activities, such as identifying cargo for examination, would not require the placement of CBP targeters in foreign ports under programs like CSI. CBP officials said they do not have plans to negotiate Customs-to-Customs MRAs because they are much more difficult to achieve than AEO-MRAs, in part, because of the difficulties in ensuring Customs practices are applied consistently. For example, CBP officials said that Customs-to-Customs MRAs would need to include a broader validation of foreign Customs administrations' practices. World Customs Organization officials we met with concurred that achieving mutual recognition of Customs controls is difficult and noted that the focus of Customs administrations worldwide is on negotiating AEO-MRAs rather than Customs-to-Customs MRAs.

CBP Has Made Efforts to Improve Efficiency and Effectiveness by Increasing CTPAT Membership

CBP has also made efforts to improve the efficiency and effectiveness of its C-TPAT program—and thus the security of the global supply chain— by increasing the number and category of C-TPAT members. For example, CBP has increased C-TPAT membership by conducting outreach events to increase awareness of the C-TPAT program and incentives. From fiscal years 2008 through 2012, the number of C-TPAT members increased by 15 percent—from 8,882 to 10,425. According to the 2013 DHS Annual Performance Report, as of fiscal year 2012, CTPAT members account for more than 50 percent of all U.S. cargo imports (by value), which exceeds CBP's performance target goal of 45 percent. Further, as part of C-TPAT's membership expansion efforts, the program is considering adding two supply chain sectors—exporters and distribution centers.[45] CBP officials reported that C-TPAT selected these sectors because they can have a direct impact in securing the global supply chain. Moreover, according to the 2012 C-TPAT Strategy Action Plan, increased membership in the C-TPAT program could allow U.S. ports of entry to operate more efficiently because CBP officials at these ports would be able to focus CBP's targeting and inspection resources on a smaller percentage of high-risk shipments.

Staffing Challenges and Members' Compliance with Security Requirements Limit CBP Efforts to Improve CTPAT Effectiveness

Although expansion of C-TPAT membership should increase program efficiencies systemwide, CBP faces challenges in increasing C-TPAT effectiveness because of staffing challenges. In particular, while the CTPAT program has continued to expand in size and scope in recent years, staffing within the program has decreased. Specifically, according to CBP officials, as of July 2013, the C-TPAT program had 155 staff, down from a peak of 196 staff in January 2011. CBP plans to take several steps to address this staffing challenge. For example, CBP officials reported that as of July 2013, C-TPAT is working with CBP's Office of Human Resources to hire 11 additional Supply Chain Security Specialists.[46] Furthermore, according to fiscal year 2014 CBP budget documentation, CBP plans to extend the C-TPAT revalidation cycle to once every 4 years as mandated by the SAFE Port Act rather than accelerating the revalidation schedule to once every 3 years as CBP had previously done. Moreover, C-TPAT officials reported that CBP anticipates a reduction in foreign validation visits by its specialists through the implementation of MRAs.

An additional challenge to C-TPAT program effectiveness is that C-TPAT partners' compliance rates with program security requirements decreased from almost 100 percent in fiscal year 2008 to about 95 percent in fiscal year 2012. According to CBP documentation, the overall compliance rate decreased after

CBP strengthened C-TPAT security criteria and increased program oversight. CBP reported that C-TPAT is working with C-TPAT partners to explain the enhanced security criteria to ensure they understand the validation requirements. CBP officials said that they expect this will lead to improvements in C-TPAT partners' compliance with the security requirements.

CBP Revised CSI in Response to Budget Cuts, but Efficiencies and Effectiveness Are Limited by Political and Legal Factors

CBP Revised CSI Targeting Approaches to Address Budget Cuts

As a result of reduced program budgets in recent years, CBP has implemented CSI changes to take advantage of improvements in technology and more efficiently use its CSI targeters, but efficiencies are limited by host country political and legal factors. Specifically, CSI program expenditures declined by more than $50 million from fiscal years 2008 through 2012, and this cut led to changes in how CBP has staffed its CSI ports. As shown in figure 5, CBP employs a variety of approaches in targeting and examining U.S.-bound containerized cargo imported from CSI countries. These targeting approaches are explained below.

National Targeting Center-Cargo (NTC-C) Support

In April 2005, we recommended that CBP revise the CSI targeting approach to consider what functions need to be performed at CSI ports and what functions can be performed in the United States.[47] CBP agreed with this recommendation and, in January 2009, began transferring some CSI staff from overseas ports to perform targeting remotely from the NTC-C. According to CBP officials, NTC-C staff are less costly than overseas staff.[48] Under this revised targeting approach, NTC-C targeters review U.S.-bound shipments from foreign ports in 6 CSI countries. For those shipments that NTC-C targeters determine to be high risk or suspect, NTC-C targeters request that host government Customs officials complete examinations and electronically provide the results to NTC-C staff. Further, according to CSI officials, NTC-C targets all shipments ATS categorizes as lower risk in an additional 6 CSI countries so that CSI targeters in those 6 countries can concentrate their reviews on the higher-risk shipments. According to CBP officials, implementation of this targeting approach allows CBP to staff high-volume ports with fewer CSI targeters. Our analysis of CSI staffing data shows that staffing of CBP targeters that support CSI at the NTC-C increased by 56 percent from fiscal years 2009 through 2012—from 27 to 42. Changes in CBP's staffing of in-country targeters are discussed below.

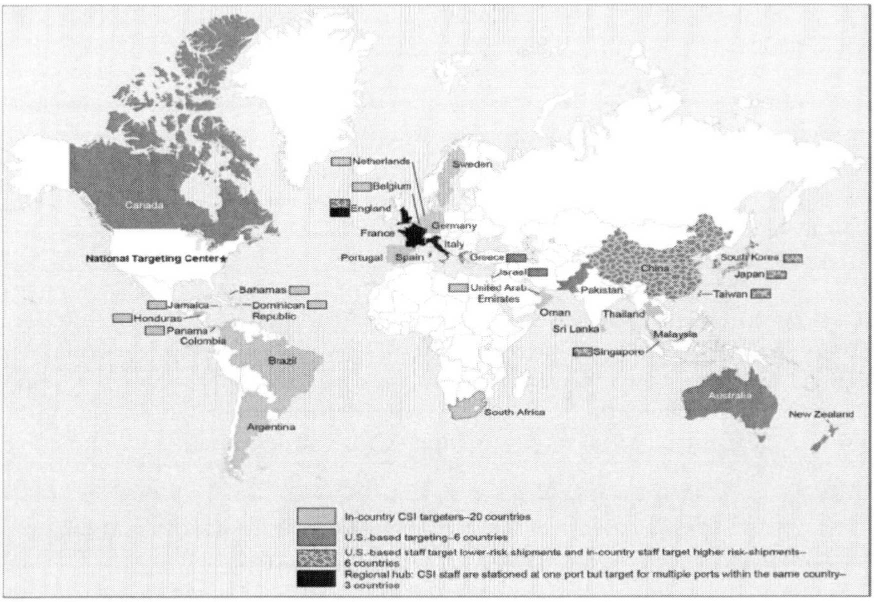

Source: GAO; Map Resources (map).

Notes: Targeting refers to the review of shipment data and additional information by CBP officials to identify high-risk shipments with a potential nexus to terrorism.

CSI ports in England utilize both the regional hub and a mixture of in-country and U.S.-based targeting approaches.

CBP coordinates targeting of U.S.-bound cargo container shipments in 34 countries that covers 61 foreign ports.

Figure 5. Map Showing the Variety of Targeting Approaches Customs and Border Protection Uses in Container Security Initiative Countries as of July 2013.

Regional Hub Model

In 2011 and 2012, CBP implemented a regional hub model whereby CSI targeters are stationed at one port but target for multiple ports within the same country to reduce staff and thereby increase efficiencies. Under this targeting approach, host government Customs officials at remote ports complete the container examinations and electronically provide the results to CSI targeters at the regional hub. According to CBP host government officials, implementation of the regional hub is possible because of improvements in technology that allow for better and more timely transmission of image scans. Of the 13 countries with multiple CSI ports, 3 employ the regional hub model— England, France, and Italy. CBP officials reported that since implementing the regional hub model, CBP has reduced the number of CSI targeters in these 3 countries by 45 percent—from 20 in October 2011 to 11 as of April 2013. According to both CBP targeters stationed in England and their British counterparts, implementation of the regional hub model has not affected the quality or number of scans of U.S.-bound container shipments.

Although implementation of the regional hub model increases efficiencies, CBP officials stated that they do not have plans to implement the regional hub model in other countries in the near future because of host country political and legal reasons. For example, CBP officials told us that CBP considered implementing the regional hub model in one country;

however, the host government preferred to maintain the face-to-face interaction between the CSI targeters and their host government counterparts at each CSI port as a means to improve information exchanges and increase collaboration. Further, according to CBP and government officials in one country, a national law precludes the transmission of electronic scanned images other than to host government Customs officials. As a result, CSI targeters must be present at each CSI port in order to view the scanned container images.

In-Country CSI Targeters

Where possible, CBP has shifted from the initial CSI targeting approach that was heavily dependent on the placement of targeters at foreign ports to an approach that takes advantage of improvements in technologies for transmitting image scans, as addressed earlier. Specifically, from fiscal years 2009 through 2012, CBP reduced the number of CSI targeters stationed at foreign ports by 50 percent—from 153 to 77. However, as noted above, CBP increased the number of CSI targeters stationed at the NTC-C during the same time period. CBP maintains in-country targeters in 20 of the 34 CSI countries. A key benefit of maintaining CSI targeters at these ports is the relationship built with host government counterparts. CSI targeters in all 6 foreign countries we visited and host government officials in 5 of the 6 countries we visited told us that personal relationships and trust that are established between CSI targeters and host country government officials from having the CSI targeters in country are fundamental to the success of the CSI program.[49] In particular, the CSI targeters and host government officials in these 5 countries agree that the physical presence of CSI staff increases information sharing and improves collaboration. Further, host country Customs officials in 3 of the 6 countries we visited stated that the presence of CSI targeters contributed to the development or enhancement of their countries' cargo targeting programs.

According to our review of CBP performance data, changes in staffing levels in recent years have not negatively affected the effectiveness of the CSI program. In particular, CBP tracks two performance measures—(1) the percentage of U.S.-bound cargo container shipments that are reviewed by CSI targeters and (2) the percentage of U.S.-requested cargo examinations that are completed by host countries. According to CBP data from fiscal years 2009 through 2012, CSI targeters met their target goal of reviewing 100 percent of the U.S.-bound cargo shipments. Moreover, the percentage of U.S.-requested examinations of U.S.-bound cargo shipments completed by host countries increased from 93 percent in fiscal year 2009 to 98 percent in fiscal year 2012, although CBP did not meet the target goal of 100 percent. CBP reported that CSI relies on the voluntary cooperation of host nation Customs officials and that CBP works with the host ports to resolve examination issues as they arise in an effort to increase the percentage of U.S.-bound shipments that are examined.

CBP Has Made Efforts to Expand the Scope of CSI beyond WMD to Improve Effectiveness

CBP has made efforts to expand the scope of CSI targeting beyond WMD, where possible, in an effort to increase the effectiveness of the CSI program. While the priority focus of CSI is to prevent WMD and other terrorist contraband from entering the United States through cargo containers, the April 2011 CSI Statement of Policy and Intent prioritized expanding the scope of CSI beyond WMD, among other things. In particular, according to the CSI Strategy Action Plan, as well as CSI program officials with whom we met, CBP is negotiating with government officials in foreign countries where CBP has CSI targeters to expand the focus of CSI's targeting efforts beyond WMD to include other contraband, such as illicit drugs, illegal weapons, and counterfeit goods (intellectual property right violations). The CBP officials we met with noted, however, that expanding the scope of CSI targeting efforts beyond WMD is ultimately at the discretion of the host governments with whom CBP has negotiated guidelines for CSI program operations. While two of the six CSI countries that we visited allow CSI staff to target U.S.-bound cargo container shipments for contraband other than WMD, the remaining four countries generally limit targeting and examinations to cargo containers suspected of containing WMD. Government officials from one of these four countries stated it is CBP's responsibility to scan containers for other suspected contraband, such as illicit drugs, once the containers arrive in the United States. Customs officials from another one of these four countries stated they do not have the resources to devote to scanning U.S.-bound containers that may be at risk for containing contraband other than WMD. According to CBP officials, though, expanding the scope of targeting at foreign ports by its CSI targeters has not resulted in additional costs to CBP in terms of numbers of targeters or funding.

CONCLUSION

Reducing risks to the global maritime supply chain is critical because foreign ports and the cargo carried by vessels from these ports are vital to the U.S. economy. DHS has made progress in reducing some maritime supply chain risks through its various maritime container security programs. The Coast Guard has developed a port security risk model that it annually updates and uses to assess port facility security, inform operational decisions, and direct resources. In contrast, CBP has not assessed the risks of foreign ports that ship cargo to the United States to determine whether its existing CSI locations remain valid since 2005. Although there have been no known incidents of cargo containers being used to transport WMD, the maritime supply chain remains vulnerable to attacks. We recognize that it may not be possible to include all of the higher-risk ports in CSI because CSI requires the cooperation of sovereign foreign governments. However, DHS and GAO risk management practices state that agencies should periodically evaluate the effectiveness of their programs and that mechanisms should be in place for altering a program based on current risk data. Periodically assessing the risk level of cargo shipped from foreign ports and using the results of these risk assessments to inform any future expansion of CSI to additional locations as well as determining whether changes need to be made to existing CSI ports would help ensure that CBP is allocating its resources to provide the greatest possible coverage of high-risk cargo to best mitigate the risk of importing WMD or other terrorist contraband into the United States through the maritime supply chain.

Recommendations for Executive Action

To better ensure the effectiveness of the CSI program, we recommend that the Secretary of Homeland Security direct the Commissioner of U.S. Customs and Border Protection to periodically assess the supply chain security risks from all foreign ports that ship cargo to the United States and use the results of these risk assessments to (1) inform any future expansion of CSI to additional locations and (2) determine whether changes need to be made to existing CSI ports and make adjustments as appropriate and feasible.

Agency Comments and Our Evaluation

In August 2013, we requested comments on a draft of this report from the Departments of Homeland Security and State. Both departments provided technical comments, which we have incorporated into the report, as appropriate. In addition to its technical comments, DHS provided an official letter for inclusion in the report. In its letter, DHS stated it concurred with the recommendation and plans to develop a process for conducting periodic assessments of the supply chain security risks from all ports that ship cargo to the United States and use information from the assessments to determine if future expansion or adjustments to CSI locations are appropriate.

Stephen L. Caldwell
Director
Homeland Security and Justice

Appendix I: Information on Foreign Ports That Coordinate Maritime Cargo Container Security Efforts with U.S. Customs and Border Protection

This appendix provides information on the foreign ports that either participate directly in the Container Security Initiative (CSI) program or that U.S. Customs and Border Protection (CBP) otherwise coordinates with to review and secure U.S.-bound cargo container shipments. As of July 2013, CBP was coordinating targeting of U.S.-bound cargo container shipments with 61 foreign ports. Table 2 lists these ports according to the date the ports began conducting operations with CBP and also provides information on, among other things, the volume of U.S.-bound shipments passing through the seaport in fiscal year 2012 and the targeting approach employed.

Table 2. Foreign Ports That CBP Coordinates with Regarding Maritime Container Shipment Examinations, as of July 2013 (Listed by Date Port Began CSI Operations)

	Seaport	Country	Date port began CSI operations	Number of U.S.-bound maritime container shipments (fiscal year 2012)	Targeting approach
1	Vancouver	Canada	2/20/2002	75,226	Remotea
2	Halifax	Canada	3/25/2002	11,731	Remote
3	Montreal	Canada	3/25/2002	257	Remote
4	Rotterdam	Netherlands	9/2/2002	177,448	In-countryb
5	Le Havre	France	12/2/2002	130,577	Regional hubc
6	Bremerhaven	Germany	2/2/2003	379,662	In-country
7	Hamburg	Germany	2/9/2003	184,163	In-country
8	Antwerp	Belgium	2/23/2003	268,479	In-country
9	Singapore	Singapore	3/10/2003	428,730	NTC-C supportd
10	Yokohama	Japan	3/24/2003	42,953	In-country
11	Hong Kong	China	5/5/2003	938,821	NTC-C support
12	Gothenburg	Sweden	5/23/2003	14,007	In-country
13	Felixstowe	United Kingdom	5/24/2003	54,926	Regional hub/NTC-Csupport
14	Genoa	Italy	6/16/2003	151,464	Regional hub
15	La Spezia	Italy	6/23/2003	139,382	Regional hub
16	Busan	South Korea	8/4/2003	867,627	NTC-C support
17	Durban	South Africa	12/1/2003	11,807	In-country
18	Port Kelang	Malaysia	3/8/2004	7,393	In-country
19	Tokyo	Japan	5/21/2004	139,659	NTC-C support
20	Piraeus	Greece	7/27/2004	9,746	Remote
21	Algeciras	Spain	7/30/2004	33,733	In-country
22	Kobe	Japan	8/6/2004	77,790	In-country
23	Nagoya	Japan	8/6/2004	74,402	In-country
24	Laem Chabang	Thailand	8/13/2004	95,551	In-country
25	Tanjung Pelepas	Malaysia	8/16/2004	84,337	In-country
26	Naples	Italy	9/30/2004	19,024	Regional hub
27	Liverpool	United Kingdom	10/19/2004	35,273	Regional hub/NTC-C support

Table 2. (Continued)

	Seaport	Country	Date port began CSI operations	Number of U.S.-bound maritime container shipments (fiscal year 2012)	Targeting approach
28	Thamesport	United Kingdom	10/19/2004	27,818	Regional hub/NTC support
29	Southampton	United Kingdom	10/19/2004	50,357	Regional hub/NTC-C support
30	Tilbury	United Kingdom	10/19/2004	2,382	Regional hub/NTC-C support
31	Gioai Tauro	Italy	10/29/2004	12,381	Regional hub
32	Zeebrugge	Belgium	10/29/2004	25	In-countrye
33	Livorno	Italy	12/16/2004	77,299	Regional hub
34	Marseilles	France	1/7/2005	16,378	Regional hub
35	Dubai	United Arab Emirates	3/26/2005	13,350	In-country
36	Shanghai	China	4/12/2005	1,900,294	NTC-C support
37	Shenzhen	China	6/24/2005	1,475,210	NTC-C support
38	Kaohsiung	Taiwan	7/25/2005	630,732	NTC-C support
39	Santos	Brazil	9/21/2005	50,816	In-country
40	Colombo	Sri Lanka	9/29/2005	127,432	In-country
41	Buenos Aires	Argentina	11/17/2005	20,791	In-country
42	Lisbon	Portugal	12/14/2005	36,903	In-country
43	Port Salalah	Oman	3/8/2006	97,450	In-country
44	Puerto Cortes	Honduras	3/25/2006	67,996	In-country
45	Aucklandf	New Zealand	4/1/2006	47,244	Remote
46	Chi-lung	Taiwan	9/25/2006	97,476	In-country
47	Valencia	Spain	9/25/2006	106,118	In-country
48	Caucedo	Dominican Republic	9/26/2006	24,843	In-country
49	Barcelona	Spain	9/27/2006	41,763	In-country
50	Kingston	Jamaica	9/28/2006	75,607	In-country
51	Freeport	Bahamas	9/29/2006	66,912	In-country
52	Qasim	Pakistan	4/30/2007	46,486	Remote
53	Shekou	Chinaf	08/01/2007	60,019	NTC-C support
54	Chiwan	China	8/1/2007	138,069	NTC-C support
55	Balboa	Panama	8/27/2007	76,380	In-country
56	Cartagena	Colombia	9/13/2007	52,682	In-country
57	Ashdod	Israel	9/17/2007	543	Remote
58	Haifa	Israel	9/25/2007	36,490	Remote

	Seaport	Country	Date port began CSI operations	Number of U.S.-bound maritime container shipments (fiscal year 2012)	Targeting approach
59	Colon	Panama	9/28/2007	50,481	In-country
60	Manzanillo	Panama	9/28/2007	77,030	In-country
61	Melbourne[f]	Australia	11/1/2011	37,730	Remote

Source: GAO presentation of CBP data.

[a]The remote targeting approach relies on host government Customs officials to complete the container examinations and electronically provide the results of any container image scans to U.S.- based CBP targeters.

[b]The in-country targeting approach places CBP targeters at CSI ports, who directly coordinate with host government Customs officials to examine containers and obtain the results of the examinations.

[c]Under the regional hub targeting approach, CSI staff are stationed at one port but target for multiple ports within the same country to increase efficiencies. Host government Customs officials at remote ports complete the container examinations and electronically provide the results to CSI targeters at the regional hub.

[d]The National Targeting Center-Cargo (NTC-C) targeting approach relies on in-country CBP targeters to review higher-risk shipments and U.S.-based CBP targeters to review lower-risk shipments. NTC-C analyzes advance cargo information before shipments reach the United States.

[e]According to CBP officials, CSI targeters in Antwerp also target U.S.-bound container shipments exported from Zeebrugge and drive to that port to participate in examinations, as necessary.

[f]According to CBP officials, CBP entered into arrangements with New Zealand and Australia to remotely target U.S.-bound cargo container shipments from Auckland and Melbourne, respectively. Further, in August 2007, CBP began targeting containers at Shenzhen, China, that did not originally participate in CSI. According to CBP officials, CSI targeters in Shenzhen are also able to review and target shipments from Shekou, China, and can drive to that port to witness examinations. For the purposes of this report, we consider a port to be a CSI port if CBP has entered into an arrangement or otherwise coordinates with a foreign country to target U.S.-bound cargo container shipments from that port. Accordingly, we consider the number of CSI ports to be 61 rather than 58.

End Notes

[1] U.S. Department of Transportation, Research and Innovative Technology Administration, Bureau of Transportation Statistics, *America's Container Ports: Linking Markets at Home and Abroad* (Washington, D.C.: January 2011).

[2] The White House, *National Strategy for Global Supply Chain Security* (Washington, D.C.: January 2012).

[3] See, for example, the *National Strategy to Combat Weapons of Mass Destruction* (Washington, D.C.: December 2002), the *National Strategy for Maritime Security* (Washington, D.C.: September 2005), the *Strategy to Enhance International Supply Chain Security* (Washington, D.C.:2007), the *National Security Strategy* (May 2010), the *National Strategy for Counterterrorism* (Washington, D.C.: June 2011), and the *National Strategy to Combat Transnational Organized Crime* (Washington, D.C.: July 2011).

[4] Risk management is a strategy called for by federal law and presidential directive and is meant to help policy makers and program officials most effectively mitigate risk while allocating limited resources under conditions of uncertainty.

[5] Pub. L. No. 107-295, 116 Stat. 2064.

[6] See 46 U.S.C. § 70116.

[7] 46 U.S.C. § 70108.

[8] Pub. L. No. 109-347, 120 Stat. 1884.

[9] For the purposes of this report, we used the following DHS definition of risk: the potential for an unwanted outcome resulting from an incident, event, or occurrence, as determined by its likelihood and the associated consequences. For example, risk is the expected consequences associated with a terrorist organization smuggling a WMD into a container at a foreign port and detonating that weapon in the United States.

[10] These key elements are contained in DHS, *National Infrastructure Protection Plan, Partnering to Enhance Protection and Resiliency* (Washington, D.C.: January 2009).

[11] GAO, *Risk Management: Further Refinements Needed to Assess Risks and Prioritize Protective Measures at Ports and Other Critical Infrastructure,* GAO-06-91 (Washington, D.C.: Dec. 15, 2005). Our prior work identified a risk management framework that we used to evaluate activities related to homeland security and combating terrorism.

[12] Transshipped containers are those that are unloaded from vessels at ports and are then reloaded to different vessels.

[13] Through MRAs with other partners, the security-related practices and programs taken by the customs or maritime security administration of one country are recognized and accepted by the administration of another. These arrangements are discussed in more detail later in this report.

[14] We also interviewed U.S. Immigration and Customs Enforcement officials regarding the Global Shield initiative to stem the illegal flow of precursor chemicals used in improvised explosive devices (IED), but we determined this program was outside the scope of this review because it is an international initiative, not a U.S. maritime security program. Global Shield is a World Customs Organization initiative in collaboration with the United Nations Office on Drugs and Crime and Interpol. Since its initiation in October 2010, more than 80 participating countries have monitored the import and export of 14 explosive precursor chemicals—identified as those most prevalently used in IEDs—around the world, in order to secure the global supply chain.

[15] According to CBP officials, CBP entered into arrangements with New Zealand (April 2006) and Australia (November 2011) to remotely target U.S.-bound cargo container shipments from Auckland and Melbourne, respectively. Further, in August 2007, CBP began targeting containers at Shenzhen, China, that did not originally participate in CSI. According to CBP officials, CSI targeters in Shenzhen are also able to review and target shipments from Shekou, China, and can drive to that port to witness examinations. For the purposes of this report, we consider a port to be a CSI port if CBP has entered into an arrangement or

otherwise coordinates with a foreign country to target U.S.-bound cargo container shipments from that port. Accordingly, we consider the number of CSI ports to be 61 rather than 58. Appendix I provides a complete listing of the 61 CSI ports.

[16] GAO, *Supply Chain Security: CBP Works with International Entities to Promote Global Customs Security Standards and Initiatives, but Challenges Remain*, GAO-08-538 (Washington, D.C.: Aug. 15, 2008).

[17] GAO-08-538.

[18] GAO-08-538.

[19] The IPS program uses the ISPS Code as the benchmark by which it measures the effectiveness of a country's antiterrorism measures in a port. The code was developed after the September 11, 2001, terrorist attacks to establish measures to enhance the security of ships and port facilities with a standardized and consistent security framework. The ISPS Code requires facilities to conduct an assessment to identify threats and vulnerabilities and then develop security plans based on the assessment. The requirements of this code are performance-based; therefore, compliance can be achieved through a variety of security measures.

[20] Conditions of entry may include restricting a vessel's movement within U.S. ports or requiring the vessel to take additional security measures, such as stationing guards at each access point of the ship when in a U.S. port.

[21] U.S. Coast Guard, *International Port Security Program: Annual Report 2012* (Washington, D.C.: March 31, 2012).

[22] MRAs can be entered into with other countries as well as other governing bodies, such as the European Union. For the purposes of this report, the countries and governing bodies that enter into MRAs with the United States are considered "partners."

[23] The World Customs Organization is an intergovernmental organization representing the customs administrations of 179 countries, which aims to enhance the effectiveness and efficiency of Customs administrations.

[24] AEOs include, for example, manufacturers, importers, exporters, brokers, ports, airports, terminal operators, warehouses, and distributors.

[25] 6 U.S.C. § 981. This pilot was called the Secure Freight Initiative. A similar cargo-scanning requirement was enacted that same year by the Department of Homeland Security Appropriations Act, 2007 (Pub. L. No. 109-295, 120 Stat. 1355 (2006)) and is codified at 6 U.S.C. § 981a. Both statutes specify scanning as examination with both radiation detection equipment and nonintrusive imaging equipment. 6 U.S.C. §§ 981(a), 981a(a)(1).

[26] Pub. L. No. 110-53, § 1701(a), 121 Stat. 266, 489-90 (amending 6 U.S.C. § 982(b)). Radiation detection equipment detects radiation being emitted from a container, and through a nonintrusive image scan, CBP can identify anomalies in a container's image that could, among other things, indicate the presence of dense material used to shield radioactive material.

[27] GAO, *Supply Chain Security: Challenges to Scanning 100 Percent of U.S.-Bound Cargo Containers*, GAO-08-533T (Washington, D.C.: June 12, 2008), and *Supply Chain Security: Feasibility and Cost-Benefit Analysis Would Assist DHS and Congress in Assessing and Implementing the Requirement to Scan 100 Percent of U.S.-Bound Containers*, GAO-10-12 (Washington, D.C.: Oct. 30, 2009).

[28] GAO, *Supply Chain Security: Container Security Programs Have Matured, but Uncertainty Persists over the Future of 100 Percent Scanning*, GAO-12-422T (Washington, D.C.: Feb. 7, 2012).

[29] The 9/11 Act scanning provision includes possible extensions for containers loaded at a port or ports for which DHS certifies that at least two out of a list of specific conditions exist.

Among others, these conditions include the following: (1) adequate scanning equipment is not available or cannot be integrated with existing systems, (2) a port does not have the physical characteristics to install the equipment, or (3) use of the equipment will significantly affect trade capacity and the flow of cargo. See 6 U.S.C. § 982(b)(4). The 9/11 Act also requires DHS to submit a report to Congress on whether it expects to seek to renew the extension 1 year after it takes effect. See id. § 982(b)(7). As of July 2013, DHS has not provided this report to Congress.

[30] DHS, *Scanning of Maritime Cargo Containers: Fiscal Year 2012 Report to Congress* (Washington, D.C.: May 3, 2012).

[31] The White House, *National Strategy for Global Supply Chain Security Implementation Update* (Washington, D.C.: January 2013).

[32] 46 U.S.C. § 70108(d).

[33] According to CBP officials, because of logistical factors such as the time necessary for negotiations with host governments and staffing CSI teams in foreign countries, initial CSI ports selected on the basis of volume sometimes did not begin operations until the expansion of CSI was under way.

[34] According to CBP officials, CBP entered into arrangments with New Zealand (April 2006) and Australia (November 2011) to remotely target U.S.-bound cargo container shipments from Auckland and Melbourne, respectively. Further, in August 2007, CBP began targeting containers at Shenzhen, China, that did not originally participate in CSI. According to CBP officials, CSI targeters in Shenzhen are also able to review and target shipments from Shekou, China, and can drive to that port to witness examinations. For the purposes of this report, we consider a port to be a CSI port if CBP has entered into an arrangement or otherwise coordinates with a foreign country to target U.S.-bound cargo container shipments from that port. Accordingly, we consider the number of CSI ports to be 61 rather than 58.

[35] GAO, *Supply Chain Security: Examinations of High-Risk Cargo at Foreign Seaports Have Increased, but Improved Data Collection and Performance Measures Are Needed,* GAO-08-187 (Washington, D.C.: Jan. 25, 2008).

[36] The original pilot locations were Busan, South Korea; Puerto Cortes, Honduras; Qasim, Pakistan, Salalah, Oman; Southampton, United Kingdom; and Hong Kong.

[37] DOE established the Megaports Initiative in 2003 to deter, detect, and interdict nuclear or other radiological materials smuggled through foreign ports. The initiative funds the installation of radiation detection equipment at select ports overseas and trains host country personnel to use this equipment to scan cargo containers entering and leaving these ports—regardless of destination. The Megaports Initiative was intended to complement the CSI program. See GAO, *Combating Nuclear Smuggling: Megaports Initiative Faces Funding and Sustainability Challenge,* GAO-13-37 (Washington, D.C.: Oct. 31, 2012).

[38] Fiscal year 2012 data were not available for 67 of the 356 ports in the 2009 model and were excluded from the analysis. However, only 3 of these ports were ranked among the top 100 riskiest ports, In addition, 3 CSI ports had fewer than 1,000 U.S.-bound shipments in fiscal year 2012 and were therefore not included in the analysis. We reached 138 ports with at least 1,000 U.S.-bound shipments instead of the 187 determined by CBP because we used fiscal year 2012 shipment data instead of the data included in the 2009 risk model

[39] 9 U.S.C. § 945(b).

[40] DHS, *National Infrastructure Protection Plan, Partnering to Enhance Protection and Resiliency* (Washington, D.C.: January 2009).

[41] See GAO-06-91.

[42] Coast Guard officials visit foreign ports to evaluate their antiterrorism security measures against established ISPS Code standards.

[43] According to DHS officials, the European Union characterizes its port visits as "inspections."

[44] The study did not account for any costs associated with negotiating the MRAs. C-TPAT has not conducted any cost studies related to the MRAs with Jordan, New Zealand, Taiwan, South Korea, or the European Union.

[45] As of July 2013, C-TPAT membership is spread over 10 different supply chain sectors, such as importers and port operators.

[46] Supply Chain Security Specialists are responsible for responding to the needs of CTPAT partners, as well as conducting training and outreach efforts with local law enforcement, CBP components, and other entities.

[47] GAO, *Container Security: A Flexible Staffing Model and Minimum Equipment Requirements Would Improve Overseas Targeting and Inspection Efforts*, GAO-05-557 (Washington, D.C.: Apr. 26, 2005).

[48] NTC-C analyzes advance cargo information using ATS prior to U.S.-bound cargo being loaded on to vessels in foreign ports. NTC-C also promotes information sharing with other federal agencies and foreign governments to detect and address threats at U.S. and foreign ports.

[49] Officials in one foreign country we visited stated that in-country CBP targeters were not important for successful CSI operations.

INDEX

#

A

B

C

D

E

F

G

H

I

J

K

L

M

S

T

U

V

W